CU00694931

Walk with Me

**Other Loyola Press books
by Nicole Gausseron**

Believe That I Am Here
The Notebooks of Nicole Gausseron:
Book One

I Am with You Always
The Notebooks of Nicole Gausseron:
Book Three

Walk
with Me

The Notebooks
of Nicole Gausseron
BOOK TWO

Translated from the French by
William Skudlarek, O.S.B., and Hilary Thimmesh, O.S.B.

LOYOLAPRESS.

CHICAGO

LOYOLAPRESS.

3441 N. ASHLAND AVENUE
CHICAGO, ILLINOIS 60657
(800) 621-1008
WWW.LOYOLABOOKS.ORG

This book, published in three volumes, is a revised, reedited, and sub-
stantially expanded version of *The Little Notebooks* originally published as one volume in 1996 in the United States by HarperCollins.

All Scripture quotations are from the New Revised Standard Version
Bible: Catholic Edition, copyright © 1993 and 1989 by the Division of
Christian Education of the National Council of the Churches of Christ
in the U.S.A. Used by permission. All rights reserved.

Cover and interior design by Judine O'Shea
Cover photo: © Robert Everts/Getty Images

Library of Congress Cataloging-in-Publication Data
Gausseron, Nicole.
  Believe that I am here : the notebooks of Nicole Gausseron / translated
from the French by William Skudlarek and Hilary Thimmesh.
      p. cm.
Rev. ed. of: The little notebook.
  ISBN 0-8294-1621-8
  1. Gausseron, Nicole—Diaries. 2. Catholics—France—Diaries. 3.
Visions. 4. Jesus Christ—Apparitions and miracles—France—Chartres.
5. Compagnons du Partage. 6. Church work with the homeless—
France—Chartres. 7. Chartres (France)—Church history—20th
century. I. Gausseron, Nicole. Little notebook. II. Title.
  BX4705.G2636A3 2003
  282'.092—dc21

                                                          2003012152

Printed in the United States of America
03 04 05 06 07 08 09 10 M-V 10 9 8 7 6 5 4 3 2 1

Across the green fields of the Beauce, the rich wheat-growing region of France southwest of Paris, the famous silhouette of the cathedral of Notre-Dame de Chartres has beckoned to pilgrims for eight hundred years. Americans are likely to identify Chartres with the cathedral. To the people who live there, however, the city is not only the site of that great medieval structure but also a bustling regional center with typical modern economic and social problems, among them the needs of the poor.

Concern for the poor, particularly the homeless men who somehow survive on the fringes of society, led a woman of Chartres to help establish and to become the first director of a home for such men in 1981. She called it the Compagnons du Partage, a phrase not very satisfactorily translated as "Companions in Sharing." She started on a shoestring, aided by Bernard Dandrel—who would later found the first European food bank—and the first year in particular was touch and go.

The woman's name was Nicole Gausseron. She came from a distinguished family and was well educated. In fact she held a degree in British literature and taught for a time before her marriage to Philippe Gausseron. They both possessed that mix of intelligence and style that is characteristically French: understated, responsible, serious, but also attuned to warm friendship and the joy of living.

At the time that Nicole started her home for homeless men she was in her late thirties, and she and Philippe had three children—Laurette, Benoît, Thierry—ages seven to eleven. She had recently had the charismatic experience of baptism in the Holy Spirit, and she had come to know the poor through volunteer service with Secours Catholique, a national charitable organization of the French Catholic Church, of which Philippe was for ten years the local president.

Some of the poor, she discovered, needed not only a meal but a place to live and work, at least for a time. She set about providing such a place. The mayor of Chartres made an unused barracks on the edge of town available rent-free. Friends and well-wishers contributed odds and ends of furniture. The first day the doors were open, three men moved in; the second day, seven more. The Compagnons du Partage was off to a shaky start and depended on Nicole's constant attention to keep going.

The story of the Compagnons du Partage is more complicated than that, of course, but it is only partly the story of *The Notebooks of Nicole Gausseron,* which begins about four years after the founding of the Companions and transforms Nicole's experience into a universal and timeless story. Struggling to care for her two communities, as she calls them—her family and the men who came to live at the Companions—and always with inadequate resources, she was on the brink of abandoning her efforts after nine months of struggle when Pierre Maghin came to live with the Companions. Pierre was a priest of the Archdiocese of Paris who, with his bishop's blessing, had become a worker-priest in the late sixties. Bernard Dandrel had met him at a charismatic prayer meeting in Chartres and had approached him about becoming the director of the Community. On the day that he reserved the Sacrament in a makeshift chapel, Nicole knew the Compagnons du Partage would continue. It was for her the beginning of a new relationship with Jesus. In the celebration of the Eucharist in this modest setting, Jesus revealed his presence as a living person with feelings of his own, as a friend sharing her burdens and her joys, as the Lord speaking to her and to others through her about their indispensable part in his kingdom.

The Notebooks of Nicole Gausseron is a record of her encounters with Jesus, kept day by day in her *petit cahier,* her little notebook. The *Notebooks,* which are published in three volumes in this English edition, cover twelve years in Nicole's life, from the mid-1980s to the late 1990s. Book One, *Believe That I Am Here,* records the entries she made from March 22, 1985, to February 4, 1986. Book Two, *Walk with Me,* picks up where the first left off and takes us through the next five years, from February 5, 1986, to May/June 1991. The final volume, *I Am with You Always,* contains the entries she made between July 1992 and March 1997. The outward events of those years are lively, as the notebooks reveal—during that time Nicole raised a family while engaging in a demanding ministry to homeless men. We read of many joys—and a full measure of sorrow—in her life. But of even greater interest is the record Nicole kept of her inner life, especially the unfolding of her relationship with her friend Jesus.

A few words about how to read the *Notebooks* may be helpful. They are first of all virtually devoid of the reverential tone that we are accustomed to in works of piety. The style is much more like that of the Gospel accounts of Jesus' ministry—episodic, terse, objective. Continuity results from the development of central themes rather than sustained narrative. This method is incremental. It builds to something of great substance and consistency, but the reader can only know that—as Nicole came to know it—by starting with slight and fragmentary impressions.

Impressions is a key word. Nicole is not a visionary. In one of her first entries in the *Notebooks* she observes that the Lord is "seated beside us" but that "It's not a shadow or an apparition, but a presence." She often gives this presence a visual form and a location but never a detailed description.

The *Notebooks* present neither visions nor special revelations. Quite the contrary, Nicole earns a firm rebuff whenever she pushes the boundary of divine omniscience. "Is there a hell?" she asks, and Jesus replies, "Why are you so concerned about my Father's affairs?" She would like to know what will become of some unfortunate men, and Jesus tells her, "Do not try to know everything." This steadfast refusal to traffic in inside information about the spiritual realm, to claim privileged insights or private revelations, is to our minds one of the strongest arguments for the authenticity of these journals. The words of Jesus that Nicole reports tell us no more than the Gospels tell us.

The value of the *Notebooks* lies in their cogent reminder of how much the Gospels do tell us about Jesus and about ourselves in relation to him. There is nothing imaginary or remote about the Jesus who speaks to Nicole, smiles at her, is amused by her recollection of a refrain from an old love song, shows just a hint of weariness in reassuring her of his love for the umpteenth time, and once, to her astonishment, admits to a touch of jealousy. If the risk for believers is to relegate Jesus to resplendent glory as the *Kyrios,* the glorified Lord who is infinitely remote from daily life and correspondingly irrelevant, the Jesus who speaks in these pages insists on avoiding that risk by being one of us here and now. The bedrock reality is that he lives now and seeks a personal relationship with those who believe in him. This assurance is repeated and emphasized. "I am not an abstract idea or a system, but a living person." Nicole's repeated expression of concern for others occasions what is perhaps the most surprising theme in the *Notebooks,* one that may jar readers accustomed to easy pieties about serving God in one another. Jesus teaches Nicole that she must first of all respond directly to his love, attend to him, recognize his priority. She is free, as are all, to respond to him or not. He will not bind her; you don't bind those you love, and besides, he and his Father "have no need for puppets." But if she responds to his love, she must not forget him in her concern for others. In the end she can do nothing for others that he doesn't do through her, and he is also in those others, even the alcoholics who leave the Compagnons du Partage to all appearances no better off than when they came. Her responsibility and what she can do for others are limited; her relationship to Jesus is unlimited.

As Nicole continues to direct the Compagnons du Partage and to befriend the homeless and broken men who come to live and work together on the outskirts of Chartres, they, in turn, continue to reveal to her not only a Jesus who shares in the sufferings of this world but also a Jesus who loves her and all people with a love that is unconditional and unbounded.

One of the most important features of this remarkable journal is its implicit claim that a deeply personal and experiential knowledge of God goes hand in hand with deeply personal and experiential service to the poor. That claim is, of course, right at the heart of the New Testament: "How does God's love abide in anyone who has the world's goods and sees a brother or sister in need and yet refuses help?" (1 John 3:17). It is not uncommon, however, to find Christians—today as well as in times past—dividing themselves into opposing camps: those who claim to be true disciples of Jesus because they devote themselves to the spiritual life, and those who claim to be his true followers because they work for social justice. Nicole's experience of an intensely personal relationship with Jesus is grounded in her direct and loving contact with people who smell bad, who cheat, lie, and steal—even from her—and is thereby rendered all the more authentic.

Finally, a word should be said about the distinctly Catholic tone of this journal. Many, perhaps even most of, Nicole's dialogues with Jesus occur at Mass, usually in the Chapel of the Companions, where Pierre celebrates daily. Nicole often spends a half hour in prayer before the Blessed Sacrament.

Belief in the real presence of Jesus in the sacrament of the Eucharist and the act of remaining before it in an attitude of adoration provide Nicole with a way of focusing her attention and prayer. But it should also be noted that Nicole's practice of gazing at the consecrated communion wafer is more than just a method or technique for entering into a contemplative style of prayer. What it offers is a way of prolonging the act of praise and thanksgiving that is central to eucharistic worship and to the Christian life. Often she complains that it is hard to turn to praise in the midst of so much suffering. Patiently and lovingly, Jesus shows her that praise and thanksgiving are not ultimately to be located in feelings of well-being or in understanding why things are as they are but in maintaining a heart-to-heart relationship with him in spite of, and in the midst of, suffering.

Nicole's sense of the immediate presence of Jesus during the eucharistic celebration is rooted in and shaped by the Scriptures. On numerous occasions the dialogue between Nicole and Jesus is directly related to the scriptural passages that are read and meditated on in the celebration of the Eucharist. As one might guess from reading the *Notebooks,* the style of the celebration of the Eucharist in the Chapel of the Companions is quite different from the "oh-so-traditional" Sunday liturgies in her parish church. At the Community the pace is more relaxed, and there is ample opportunity for personal and spontaneous prayer. Nicole's words to Jesus are sometimes spoken aloud during these pauses for personal prayer, and on occasion Jesus asks her to convey his words to the small congregation that has come together for worship.

It may be helpful to note that the men who seek shelter at the Compagnons du Partage are welcomed in the name of Jesus but are not obliged to participate in any religious activities. The only conditions for living in the Community are that they not use drugs or alcohol and that they be willing to contribute to the work of the Community during their stay, which for most is a period of about three months. The work consists of collecting and repairing used goods and selling them in a secondhand store.

The Hermitage to which Nicole often refers is a farm about five miles from Chartres acquired in 1985 to provide more adequate living quarters for the Companions. The administrative center and place of work on the outskirts of the city is consistently referred to as the Community, and *Companion* is capitalized when it refers to a resident of the Compagnons du Partage.

In our judgment this remarkable journal modestly makes an extraordinary claim: that the Jesus of faith has given this teaching about himself to a woman of Chartres in our time. We have found that *The Notebooks of Nicole Gausseron* reveal their depths on repeated reading. When read straight through, the *Notebooks* give readers a sense of the movement of the journey that Jesus asks his followers to embark on, but each volume also rewards the random reader. On almost every page there is a word or statement that helps one understand more clearly and more concretely that a deep and personal relationship with Jesus—and, through Jesus, with God—is the heart and soul of the Christian life and that it contributes to the "weaving of the kingdom" when it is given expression in a preferential love for the poor.

William Skudlarek, O.S.B.
Hilary Thimmesh, O.S.B.

Saint John's Abbey, Collegeville, Minnesota

February 5

The first burial. At the hospital. It's poor and barren, not even a flower. We are burying the brother of one of the Companions. The poor and the homeless are there, about fifteen of them. Secours Catholique is present, too. Pierre, the Companions.

The Lord enters the church and seems to take us all in his arms.

✝ *Be joyful. You are rich in me.*

Later on there is the funeral, without Mass, of a month-old baby. The mother is in anguish. The pain that the others are suffering affects me deeply. But the baby is among the living.

✝ *Do not put your trust in yourselves. Put it in
me. You have me inside you like a buried
treasure. Entrust yourselves to me. Do what
you have to do, but lean on me.*

Beams of light seem to shine forth from his open hands.

☦ *I pour out my tenderness on you. Let it wash over you.*

It's like a great light, a sweetness that floods us.

☦ *This light is not going to melt away your difficulties. It will not make the cross you are carrying disappear. It envelops everything. Believe in my tenderness.*

I do believe in it, Jesus.

February 19

Where are you, Lord?

No answer.

A few minutes later the back of my neck begins to feel warm. It's like a bright point centered on a spot on my neck. I'm suspicious at first. I rub my hand over the spot. There's nothing there, and yet I feel this warmth until the end of Mass.

What's this all about?

✝ *I want you to feel me.*

February

There are twelve of us in the group. On the very first day I break my wrist.

> I think I'm going to have a lot of time to spend with you, Jesus.

He smiles.

I come and kneel before him, with him, in a little chapel in Abriès.

> ✝ *Continue to be my little servant. Let me work through you.*

February 23

The little chapel is closed. I walk along a snow-covered path. We speak to each other.

Why are you always calling me "little servant"?

✝ *I want you to take care of the others.*

Are you the one who will do that in me?

✝ *Yes. Let it happen.*

February 24

On a snow-covered road made brilliant by the sun.

"Little servant"? Explain that a little more.

✝ *Like Mary. Be like her.*

Is that all? The Lord has pretty high hopes!

"Little." The word sounds positive. Tell me
more.

✝ *Little servant and queen of my heart.*

What a way of life! The words shock me. Tears spring to
my eyes. Tomorrow he will explain it to me more fully.

February 25

I have been walking in the snow for an hour all by myself, in silence. He tells me what he means by "queen of my heart."

Little and queen of my heart?

✝ *That means that you will touch my heart.*
I will be touched by the things you will say
to me.

. . . ! ! ! I'll be able to ask you for absolutely anything?

✝ *No, Nicole. Little. You will be like a belt that*
transmits power from one pulley to another.
It will not be you who does the asking but the
others through you.

February 26

I look at a rushing torrent. Here and there it is blocked by piles of snow.

> ✝ *Little. That is what you are seeing, Nicole.*

The flowing water is clear and strong.

> ✝ *Yes. Take a good look at it.*

The snow on the two banks keeps the water from spreading out over the whole riverbed.

> ✝ *Do you see, Nicole? Being little means allowing yourself to be channeled by me. Do not spread yourself out. Let yourself be channeled and, like the torrent, you will be much more powerful.*

It seems that the Lord wants me to keep the water clear. He will see to it that it runs swiftly.

> You want people to see both the clarity and the power of the torrent. You want me to be like this mountain stream?

> ✝ *Yes.*

That's what I want too, but I'm not worthy.

> ✝ *Just wait. You will see.*

February 27

I'm still taking walks in these mountains that are almost too white. Suddenly, I realize that I don't hear the torrent anymore.

✠ *Bury yourself as it did. Bury yourself in me.*

What you want me to do, Jesus, is draw my strength from you, with you?

✠ *Yes.*

Early March

The Way of the Cross in a little chapel with four elderly women from the area. After each station they race through their Our Fathers and Hail Marys. It makes me dizzy, and their speed, which is almost offensive, gets on my nerves.

> They're not speaking to you, Lord. They're just churning out prayers.

He smiles and says nothing.

> And all this gloom, Lord. It's really depressing.

Still no reply. And then I realize that I'm very spoiled because I spend my life with someone who is truly alive. The Way of the Cross is behind, not ahead. I'm definitely very spoiled. I feel like a little child with an enormous Christmas present in her arms. The present is so big that I can hardly handle it. I really do have to let go.

March

The Lord asks me to be joyful. A little earlier, during a funeral Mass for the mother of a friend of our children, the Lord had already asked me to be joyful. She died after an eleven-year struggle against cancer and left a fifteen-year-old son. To all appearances her death is absurd.

> I feel so terrible for this child, and you ask me to be joyful.

> ✝ *Yes. In my loving gaze, in my gaze that sees you as you are, that creates and shapes you each day, be joyful.*

March 4

He tells me once again to be joyful. To be happy to live with him and by him.

   ✝ *Be transparent, too.*

This is a living bond that he offers me. There's nothing platonic about it.

March 6 and 7

I'm reading *Prison to Praise* by Merlin R. Carothers. It's very American, a little simplistic. Saying "thank you" in any and all circumstances rubs me the wrong way, and so I talk to the Lord about it.

✝ *To me, each and every* thank you *is unique.*

Lord, I simply cannot say "thank you" for the nails they drove into your hands. It's not possible.

He smiles.

Could you explain it to me, Lord?

✝ *I will teach you another way.*

Start right now.

✝ *Through it all, Nicole. I am with you through it all. Giles in the hospital with cancer, Lucette and her child who is undergoing psychiatric therapy, Martine and her husband who is withdrawing more and more. I know all that. Weep with them, yes. Suffer with them, Nicole, but through it all tell them that I am present, that I am there through it all.*

I don't see anything. I'll have to make this act of faith in total darkness.

✝ *Do not allow yourself to be completely swallowed up by your compassion. Save a place for me. Let me suffer with you. I am there, too.*

March 13

The back of my neck feels heavy, as if someone were pressing on it from above. The pressure is strong, but it doesn't hurt. Once again, I have the impression that I'm sinking.

What are you trying to tell me, Jesus?

✝ *Be little, obedient.*

When I'm relaxed like this, I feel fine. Like this, things seem easy.

✝ *Let go, let me do it. I want you to sense that obedience will make you happy and at ease.*

March 16

I see the face of the Lord, immense and smiling.

✝ *I have taken everything unto myself, have absorbed everything. Do not be afraid. I am here.*

March 18

This morning, while shopping, I see two Companions at a sidewalk café. They should have been back two days ago.

> Lord, what we're doing is so trifling. We're not able to hold on to them. Sooner or later they all go back to drink. It hurts.

> ✝ *It is not your community, Nicole. It is mine.*

At that very moment, I let go of everything. I handed it all over to him. He knows better than I do.

That evening at the chapel:

> ✝ *I will place my love in your heart. I will come and love in you. Do not be afraid.*

> What about me? I'm not to do anything? Just be passive? That's pretty negative, Lord.

> ✝ *No, you are to stay little and obedient. Take people and things as I give them to you and then . . . let me handle it.*

March

A miniretreat of not quite two full days. Concelebrated Mass in the basilica. The Gospel: Mary pours precious perfume on the feet of Jesus.

✝ *Do what she did.*

You want me to sit at your feet, to take time for you?

✝ *Yes, and more than that. I want you to spoil me.*

You certainly do spoil me, Lord. And I'd like to try to spoil you. But I don't have anything precious to offer you.

✝ *I need you to spoil me.*

What do I have that is precious and that I can pour out on you?

✝ *Your trust, your childlike trust. Make that your gift to me.*

I see, or rather I sense, what he means. He doesn't want a few isolated acts of confidence; he wants my faith in him to be poured out freely and continuously.

Later, when I'm alone with him in the oratory feeling warm and comfortable, I entrust to him the suffering of those who are in my care, the Community of the Companions, the difficult ones. I'm at his feet. Both of us are happy.

March

I'm seated at his feet.

> Lord, I give you my trust. But, you know, it's easy
> today; tomorrow will be more difficult. It's not
> clear how one can be caught up in the messiness
> of everyday life and still remain faithful to you.

> ✝ *No "yes, but." Give me this trust without any*
>   *holding back.*

> It's yours.

An instant of communion. He raises his face to me and, like
a lover, surrounds me with his light.

> Do you want us to be two and one at the same
> time?

> ✝ *Yes. I want to become your breathing. We will*
>   *breathe together.*

Oh . . . I wonder if the Lord isn't going a little too far.

> Do you really want to live in me?

> ✝ *Yes.*

> What is it you love in me?

> ✝ *You are fresh and calm.*

Not always, Lord. Far from it. You know how unbearable and headstrong I can be.

✝ *Yes, I know.*

He smiles.

Such love, such love for the little wisp of a woman that I am, is completely beyond my understanding.

Do you really need me?

✝ *Yes.*

I still feel like arguing, and so I do. I tell him again that I need Philippe, Pierre, Bernard, that I need human hands and human love if I'm to keep going.

He's a little pained as he answers me:

✝ *I have always spoiled you. I have always given you those hands. What makes you think I am going to stop now?*

I sense deeply that if I succeed in living and breathing with him, only the present moment will count. Fears, suffering, worry will no longer amount to anything.

Help me, Jesus. I want the promise I make to you today to be more than just a flash in the pan. See to it that when difficulty comes my way I don't try to go it alone and leave you off to the side. If I go on my way without you, catch me quickly. I know that it's only in this way that your kingdom will advance. Yes, Lord, we will breathe together. That's what I want.

The Beginning of April

These past days have been somewhat hard. Having my arm in a cast bothers me, but it's too painful to go without the cast. On top of that, I had an abscess and a tooth extracted. The sky is as gray as the month of November, and the wind is so cold that you need your winter coat and boots. I feel heavy, shriveled up.

Pierre is away, but the Community is getting along pretty well.

April

I am here to see you, Lord. I haven't been very attentive to you.

✝ *I was waiting for you.*

Just the hint of a reprimand.

I take time to spend a half hour with him by myself. The chapel is cold and deserted in Pierre's absence.

It's good to be with you, Lord.

And it's true. He warms my heart. I hear the Companions calling to one another, the door banging. I hear the sounds of life outside, but at the same time I sense another life within me.

Why am I ignoring you a little right now, Lord, even though I know you are the true life? I don't only know it, I savor it.

✝ *I am life to the full. The road I offer you is full of light. You will walk in pools of light.*

Then why am I holding back a little? Tell me.

✝ *Because you want to know things ahead of time.*

What things?

✝ *The gifts that I am giving you: my peace, my joy, my liberty.*

And what's wrong with that?

✝ *You cannot. You imagine these gifts in relation to your own experience, according to what you know about peace and joy and light. But my peace, the peace that I am giving you, comes from me. You cannot know it, because it is other.*

I imagine it to be immense and profound.

✝ *It is life to the full. You can only come to know it by letting go.*

April 8

A quiet day, on the whole. I take some time to rest with the Lord.

> This chapel is cold, Lord, and those Companions who used to be with us for the Eucharist have started drinking again. That hurts.

☩ *The point is not their fidelity, but yours.*

> How can you say that, Lord? We were in this together. You want us to be your witnesses, don't you?

☩ *A witness, yes. I want you to be a little servant and a witness to the light.*

April 9

Alone in his presence in this cold chapel, I try to forget about the day, about the suicidal Companion that I have just been listening to, in order to enter into communion with him.

Today's been tough.

✢ *Be sure of me.*

What do you mean?

He repeats:

✢ *Be sure of me, unconditionally sure of me.*

Tell me what you mean.

✢ *Be sure of me independent of the circum-*
stances I give you to live through, the people
you meet, the pleasant or difficult situations
in which you find yourself. Be sure of me,
enriched by me, regardless of what may come.

April 12

The Gospel of a few loaves of bread and some fish that fed a whole crowd. This Gospel is meant for us today.

> These few loaves of bread are so trifling, Lord.
> And I have the impression that what we're doing
> here for the Companions is trifling, too.

There are only three of us at the Eucharist. Yesterday we were two. The Companions who used to take part in this meal have left and have returned to drink, to the street, to misery.

> ✝ *Believe in the trifling. I give the increase. I do the multiplying.*

April 14

A few days of vacation, just me and Philippe. At last! I find the torrent from last February again, but this time the snow is gone and the stream is wide and shallow.

> There's a season for everything, isn't there, Lord? Now it's spring. It's the same torrent, but how different it is from that of last winter.

✝ *Do not be in a hurry. Be like the water of this stream. Give yourself over to me.*

> In other words?

✝ *Let yourself be channeled, guided by me. Be like the stream; do not go too fast. Accept these days when it seems that nothing or very little is happening in the Community. I am preparing you, getting you ready for tomorrow. You do not see much. The stream is under the snow. But I am on the job, busy at work.*

> It's true. You're helping me, helping us, to mature.

✝ *Yes. Allow me to work through you.*

April 15

The snow, the silence, and the repose are like a cocoon for me. I thank Jesus for this peaceful time with Philippe. It's such a gift.

> ✝ *Keep on letting go.*

The image of water and a torrent returns.

> ✝ *Do not confuse letting go with passivity. Be joyful and clear like this water, without worrying about where I am taking you. Do not be impatient. I know where I am leading you.*

I want to ask you where.

> ✝ *Why do you want to know? Are you afraid? Do you not trust me?*

April 16

Philippe has left for the mountains, and I come to spend a few moments with Jesus. As a way of placing myself in his presence, I often begin by saying "thank you" (for Philippe, the children, this place, and so on), and then I slowly recite the words of the Our Father and the Hail Mary. Both Jesus and Mary are present, and they're happy to see me like this. All is well.

Talk to me, Jesus. I'm sure you have something to say to me again today.

✝ *Yes. Do you remember when I mentioned the second breath?*

Yes.

✝ *It is easier than you think. Let go. Not just of a part of yourself but of your whole self.*

Tell me what you mean.

✝ *It is like when you swim. Your whole body goes forward in the water. Let yourself be completely carried by the current. Do not cling to the shore; do not go against the current.*

So what you're proposing is not some kind of passivity.

✝ *No, not at all. I am talking about obedience.*
You follow the current without knowing where
it will lead you, because you know how good
it feels to let yourself be carried by the water.
Just to swim.

What for, Jesus?

✝ *So that the world will see me.*

April 17

Today the message is very simple. The image is still that of the torrent.

> ✝ *Do not be afraid. The water carries you. I carry you.*

April 18

I am your servant. It's easy when I feel happy, rested, relaxed. Do you have something to tell me?

✝ *Only in my eternity will you see where the torrent ends. The current that moves it is the same as the one you will discover after death. There will be no more snags or rocks. You will not feel like clinging to the bank.*

April 21

Eucharist, Gospel: the shepherd leads his sheep to graze in green pastures.

We speak to each other:

> It doesn't seem to me that your pastures are always so delicate, green, or agreeable.

> ✝ *You are not a sheep. Stop looking at things at ground level.*

Later, in the chapel, I speak to him:

> You're not going to visit me any longer. It's already more than a year that we have been meeting. But it's going to come to an end, isn't it?

> ✝ *Nicole, I already have spoken to you so often, have given you so much. Now it is time to put into practice what I have told you.*

> I'll try.

Next day

✝ *I have really spoiled you.*

It's true, I know it. An image of jewelry—pearls—comes to me. The jewelry is lustrous and I'm intrigued by it.

✝ *The jewelry represents my words to you.*
These necklaces and all this finery are what
you have received and, in some sense, what
you have worn. But now, Nicole, you have to
wear this jewelry on the inside. Do you
understand?

Yes.

But I know I'm going to need time.

May 13

Gospel of St. John.

So much love overwhelms me. I glimpse something like a powerful and infinite current binding the Father to the Son.

> Thank you, Jesus, for having chosen us as your friends. Thank you for having allowed us to enter this privileged circle.

> ☩ *You are not inside the circle. You have not been invited into some kind of club. That is not what this is about. You take part in the very movement.*

> What do you mean?

He gives me the image of a triangle. The three corners are bound together by a perpetual movement going from one corner to the next. Each corner acts as a point of attraction, drawing the force of the movement. We are in the force itself. We are not on the outside or on the inside of the triangle, but a part of the force of the movement itself.

July

For a few months now, Jesus seems not so much distant as silent. After a year of dialogue that was both marvelous and disconcerting, am I now going to enter into the night?

With a smile on his face, the only thing the Lord said to me was:

> ✝ *Assimilate this little notebook, this treasure that I have given you.*

As you wish, Lord. I'm going to try . . . and to let go.

July

VACATION IN GREECE WITH PHILIPPE AND
THE CHILDREN

We backpack from island to island, happy to be together
even if once in a while we get on one another's nerves. We
each have our own likes and dislikes, and so we have to try
to compromise. In this vacation setting where the sky is
blue, a strangely limpid blue, and the sea is lovely and
gentle, it's difficult, almost impossible, to encounter him. I
feel bad and tell him so.

> ✝ *I am getting you ready. Do not worry about*
> *anything.*

But still I feel like something of an orphan. I especially feel
like a stranger among this horde of scruffy tourists who are
only interested in buying things. It's such a pagan world.

But at Patmos, in the cave where St. John wrote the
Apocalypse, I was finally able to find you, Lord. All by
myself, eyed by a Greek Orthodox priest who was afraid I
was going to steal one of the golden treasures that filled the
poor grotto, I knelt and wept. The certainty that Jesus is
living flooded me. My tears were my only prayer. St. John
would understand.

August

The Community has gotten bigger with the arrival of a hermit who is looking for the horizontal dimension of the cross—namely, contact and interaction with the poor—and of a chaplain from a psychiatric hospital who is spending a week of his vacation with us, cleaning beans and helping with the scrap iron and recyclable paper. *Sharing* is a difficult word for me. But when I saw you in your work clothes, Father Simon, becoming little in the midst of these little ones, I was able to see what sharing means.

In our two poor and barren chapels, three priests concelebrate the Eucharist every day. We are being spoiled. I find strength and comfort in the breaking of the bread. Without him, we wouldn't be here. The mission we have been entrusted with is crazy, impossible. How can we possibly help these men? All we can do is be present to them with the love that Jesus has bestowed on us. As for human solutions, we have few, very few, to offer. We don't have the time or the help to make new men out of them. Whether they're alcoholics or psychologically disturbed, at some time in the future they're going to go back to their old ways. All we are is a tiny speck of light. A little bit of a candle that lights up their night. It's so little, but it can really be a lot if Jesus wants to make a bigger light out of it. That's his part. Our part is being satisfied with being tiny little specks of light.

August

☩ *Believe in me. Believe in me, all of you.*

You're very insistent.

☩ *If you believe in me, you give me impetus. I need your faith in order to act. The élan comes from you.*

August

✝ *I am master of the impossible. Do you believe
that?*

Yes.

My *yes* is a little timid, because I don't really believe it. I
say *yes* with an obedient mind, but the rest of me says
maybe.

✝ *You do not understand. It is my impossible,
not yours.*

Hmm . . . that sounds like a bit of a pirouette,
doesn't it?

✝ *No. My impossible will amaze you.*

August

I'm amazed by what you do for me, with me, for them.

✝ *Keep on being amazed. Keep on.*

August

The Gospel about the foolish and prudent virgins.

In silence we meditate on this Gospel.

> Jesus, am I one of the foolish or one of the pru-
> dent? Is my lamp full of oil?
>
> ✝ *It is only half-full.*
>
> What do I have to do, Lord?
>
> ✝ *Nothing.*
>
> What do you mean? I don't understand, and that
> worries me.
>
> ✝ *Do not worry. Do not worry about anything.*
> *It is I who will fill your lamp.*
>
> Oh . . .

I promise myself to ask him how tomorrow. But first I have
to make what he's telling me my own.

August

I'm a bit apprehensive as I ask him after the Consecration:

Are you going to explain it to me?

✝ *Yes.*

Tell me.

✝ *You fill the first part of your lamp. I will occupy the second part, and I will even fill it to overflowing. Believe in me. I am your friend. I will protect you. All you have to do is believe from the bottom of your heart, and your lamp will be filled.*

You want me to do that, come what may?

✝ *Yes.*

It's not that easy, you know.

✝ *It is much easier than you think. Let go. Do not let anyone make you doubt. Look at everything I am giving you. Is that not enough?*

Oh yes, but . . .

✝ *Get rid of that "but."*

September 1

The hermit who has been with us for two months is leaving. This is his last Mass at the Chapel of the Companions. I entrust him to the Lord. He knows the thoughts that are upsetting me and the sadness that weighs down my soul.

Jesus comes and gently kneels in front of me and takes me in his arms. It's wonderfully comforting.

> ✝ *Believe in me. I will not abandon you.*

Then:

> ✝ *Love without any security.*

> I have the impression that all our efforts to draw people out of their misery, to draw them to you, are coming to naught.

Intellectually, I know that we're doing the right thing, that we have to love those who are down and out, but sometimes it's difficult to put it into practice.

Jesus adds:

> ✝ *I will continue to spoil you. Do not be afraid.*

September 2

In fact, Jesus was not going to put off spoiling me, because the next day, out of the blue, a friend came to the house to ask if Jean-Claude, a Franciscan priest who lives on the streets with the homeless, could celebrate Mass at our house. Of course he could.

Jean-Claude came. He's gotten very thin and his face is emaciated. My kids are captivated, and the few members from the lay community Companions of the Lamb who are also present are fascinated by him. At the Consecration the Lord comes and places his face on mine.

✝ *I told you, did I not?*

Jean-Claude gives us an hour-long teaching. I dare say he really doesn't teach me anything. I already know it. In his own way, Jesus has already made me know it inwardly. What Jean-Claude brings is a flash of lightning, strong and intense. What authority this man of God has. I'd love to share my notebook with him. Someday, perhaps.

September 3

Ever since Pierre left to preach a retreat, everything has become more difficult. The men don't like to take orders from a woman. One of the volunteers wants to be in charge, but does everything wrong. I find out that some of the Companions at the Hermitage have been drinking. I'm going to have to come down hard on them. This morning I need to remind them that none of them is to consider himself a little boss.

So here I am, once again becoming tough and blunt. But that's the way it has to be. If I don't take charge, there will soon be chaos.

✝ *Love them. Even as you do what you have to do, love them.*

It's not easy, and today, with all these proposals and activities happening at cross-purposes, I've had it.

✝ *Love them. They are weak, they are often incompetent, and they lie. Love them. That is how they are, the people I am lending you.*

September 4

I speak to him:

> Lord, I'm going to have a meeting with them,
> and I'm going to have to bawl them out because
> of this damn alcohol.

> ☦ *Bawl them out and love them at the same
> time.*

I don't think any more about what I'm going to tell them. I let myself be soothed by the sight of fields in sunlight. I love the Beauce.

The meeting: they're here and they look ill at ease. I'd like to tell them that I love them, but that's impossible. It just wouldn't work. But I say it in other words. In brief, I tell them that everyone does stupid things, including me. What you have done is pretty stupid. Admit it and let's get on with it.

The principal culprit leaves on his own without my having to ask him. He's not going to make it by himself. I tell him so and affirm my affection for him. Pierre does, too.

I know, he tells me.

The Lord made everything easy for me because deep down I'm at peace. Today, at that very moment, I was purified of all judgment about them.

Four of us are at the eucharistic service, and I thank him.

✝ *What did I tell you? Go forward. Follow me.*
   It is easy. Nothing will happen to you.

September 5

I was afraid that I was going to be all alone in the chapel, but it was nothing of the sort. Jean-Claude returned with a brother from his Franciscan community. At the moment of the Consecration I'm brutally dragged back over the centuries. The hands that raise the Host and that take and offer the wine are those of Christ. It's brutally intense, inescapable. The gestures, the words: it's happening for the first time. Today, at this moment, I'm in the chapel, and at the same time, I'm present at the Last Supper. This isn't a repetition, a "re-something." This is the real thing, the first time. With my whole being I'm present at the first meal when Jesus shared his own body and blood.

It's crazy. It's like being drunk. Dare I say that I'm "soused"? It's such a vulgar word, but that's more or less what I experience, what's granted to me.

I had no part in bringing this about. I don't deserve all these graces. I don't have words to express what's happening. What comes back to me in my heart are the words of Jesus: *I will make you a queen.*

September 6

A rich, exhausting, chopped-up day. Divided between the two locations of the Companions, the Hermitage and the Rue des Comtesses. Part of the day is taken up with a group of German friends and benefactors whom we welcome and show around. Uncle Pierre, a monk of Saint-Benoît-sur-Loire, stops in and brightens my day. I'm living in the present, moment by moment. Things are moving fast, but I promised myself that I wouldn't go into a skid or get frazzled. One thing at a time; one person at a time. By this I mean that when a Companion or someone else is talking to me, I try to focus on that person. I don't always succeed, but I'm working on it.

The little chapel is full: two Companions and some friends of the Franciscans. And here I was afraid I'd be all alone!

Jesus comes and wraps us in his tenderness, happy to see us happy.

> Thank you. You know, I can't help feeling a
> little scared when I'm all by myself at the head
> of this flock.

> ✝ *I know. Surrender yourself.*

Why do you insist on that so much? Because
you are all-powerful and can do everything?

✝ *No. I need your faith. I need you to believe in
me and to love me.*

I can't believe that you need my love.

✝ *Yes, I do. I need it to be able to act in you and
through you. Do you understand?*

What you want is a relationship?

✝ *I am alive.*

September

My son Benoît and I were talking about religion, faith, the Mass, and so on.

"What it comes down to," says Benoît, "is a kind of Socratic method that the Lord uses to guide your imagination."

"Why do you say that?"

"Because you don't hear a voice, like you hear mine, for example."

"Not exactly, but it's something distinct. He really does speak to me."

"Don't get upset, Mom. I believe you."

Sepember

Uncle Pierre is celebrating the Mass in our little chapel this morning.

I thank the Lord for being here. This time I see the image of a huge carpet being unrolled. The Lord is weaving it, and the threads intertwine. Our encounters, our lives, are the threads and the knots of the carpet. The Lord is the master of it: he does the weaving.

September

Jean-Claude and several friends.

> ✝ *Carry me with you. Take me with you. I do not take up a lot of space. Do not weigh yourselves down with anything else but me.*

September

There are two of us kneeling before the Lord and reading the Gospel of the day: the centurion who asks the Lord to cure the slave he loves.

Why this expression of admiration, Lord? Why? You know what's in the heart. Why do you admire the faith of this centurion?

✝ *Because he really believes in me. His faith is rooted in his own life. He understands that his life is my gift, and he really believes in me.*

And you're so deeply touched by that?

✝ *Yes. He really loves me.*

But why the intermediaries? Why send friends? But I don't have time now. I have to leave the chapel to see the Companions and then get dinner ready. We'll see each other tomorrow, Lord, and then you will clear it up for me.

Next day

On the way to Arcueil and the food bank, where I'm supposed to meet Bernard, a brother and a friend.

It's raining. I have to maneuver my way around some oversized trucks. I hear:

> ✝ *I will send you along other roads, the way I am doing now.*

What an idea, Lord! I'm not a very good driver. Just where is it you want to send me?

> ✝ *On the highway of people's hearts. And besides, I am the one who will do the driving.*

I can already hear Philippe: God knows what he's doing when he doesn't let you get behind the wheel. You're no queen of the road.

Bernard continues to be faithful to his commitment, despite all the work and problems that are piled on him. He, too, is in charge of a community like ours, but he's always available.

Father Arthur is here, and so it's possible for us to celebrate the Eucharist. Bernard is at my side, and when he prays he is like a child in God's presence. The Lord must delight in him. We sit down to a meal and good conversation, during which I learn that the food bank is opening many branches. On my way home the Lord begins the conversation.

✝ *Bernard is a good centurion.*

Are you continuing yesterday's conversation, Lord?

✝ *Yes. He is a good centurion. He, too, makes use of intermediaries.*

Ah . . .

Let me go back a little: when I got to the food bank, Bernard and Father Arthur were troubled. A man in Bernard's community was refusing to leave. He was having spiritual hallucinations, upsetting the community, and so on. As I listened to the two of them, it seemed like I was back in the Community of the Companions. It's a familiar story. Anyway, this difficult person shows up at Mass. We pray and share together. The poor fellow isn't doing very well. During Mass I ask the Lord to take care of him.

And then a little miracle happened, the kind that happens here. Without any effort at all, Father Arthur was able to get through to him, and he decided to leave.

Bernard calmly explained to me:

"When we have a difficult situation to resolve, I fast and pray. This morning I didn't have any breakfast. For me, that's a real sacrifice."

Little brother Bernard, good centurion, you amaze me!

Was fasting Bernard's intermediary? The friends of the centurion sent him to you. Is this case similar?

✝ *Yes. The intermediaries make it possible for me to weave my fabric along with you.*

September

Gospel: Mary Magdalene pours perfume on the feet of Jesus and weeps.

> ✝ *You see, Nicole, she also makes use of intermediaries.*

The perfume and her weeping, right?

> ✝ *Yes.*

I allow a moment of silence to come over me and I understand that the Lord wants us to use what he gives us—what he gives me—to go toward him. We have to start from what and who we are, not from some external system. The intermediaries are within our reach.

> ✝ *Love me. Allow me to love you. Let me act in you.*

> . . .

> ✝ *Love me starting with your own life, starting with everything I give you to be and to live. I will make you a queen. Remain little. Have a smile on your face. Be joyful.*

His tenderness floods over me.

September

✝ *I will make you a queen. Stay small, smiling,
and joyful.*

His tenderness washes over me.

September

✝ *Be innocent. Remain innocent.*

But that's so hard, Lord. It's because of you that I have come to recognize and experience all this human misery. You want us to be innocent in the midst of all this?

✝ *Listen, accept, sympathize, but do not allow yourself to be worn down. Keep on being innocent with me, new with me. Leave the initiative to me, as well as the carrying and the doing. Do not be afraid. Be innocent and accept everything and everyone. I will do what needs to be done.*

September 23

Once more, I'm intensely happy to be alive and to be so in touch with the world and especially with Jesus. The world in which we live is prey to violence. I have a friend who is very sick, and I'm assailed by all sorts of petty administrative problems, yet I feel such a sense of harmony in myself as I make my way to the Community. The street is as ugly as ever, the human and organizational problems that I'll have to take care of in a little while are no joke, and still I feel like singing. What a gift that is.

I say to him:

> I'm really spoiled, Lord, and I really sense that you take delight in me. But what about the others, Jesus? Why do they have less than I?
>
> ✝ *What do you know about that?*
>
> Take Philippe, for example, and others. I'm blessed with this intense dialogue with you that so many of your other friends would like to have. There are priests, sisters, many others . . .
>
> ✝ *Nicole, you are looking at the back of the tapestry that I am weaving along with you. I see it from the front. When you are with me, you will see it as I do: from the front.*

I have no desire to die right now. Not at all! Not at all!

He smiles and continues:

✝ *Do you see? It is like a painting or a picture.*
A large block of brilliant color needs a little
dot, a tiny little speck alongside it, to make
the color come alive. If that luminous little
dot is missing, the block of brilliant color will
not shimmer. Do you understand?

Yes. But I have the impression, Lord, that I'm
nothing but a big, red brushstroke.

✝ *That could be. Make this stroke shimmer.*
Make it shine out.

Then he continues:

✝ *Be content with seeing only the back of the*
tapestry. It is a bit of a mess. There are
threads all over, tangled colors, and parts left
unfinished. But all these overlapping pieces,
this jumble, produce the impression of unity
and harmony from the front. Do you under-
stand?

Yes, Lord. I'll be patient.

September

There are four of us. I feel a little distant. I need to be silent. Suddenly, I'm invaded by a sense of peace, but it's so strange, like a fierce, heavy weight that crashes down on me. I feel completely immersed, out of touch, buried and yet present. What an expression of love!

Why such great love, Lord? Why me?

✝ *It is free. Because I love you.*

I have the impression that every part of me is bathed in an incredible tenderness. It's almost too much. I tell him so.

✝ *Really, Nicole? Why do you not simply accept the gracious gift of my love?*

Because, because . . . I'd like to give you something in return. We're not equals. I don't deserve it. . . .

I realize that I'm getting all mixed up, and then suddenly everything becomes clear. He tells me:

✝ *Be little.*

Yes, everything becomes clear. We're not talking about becoming little by willing to be so, by obedience, by a decision. No, this is a littleness that comes about as a result of something else. God's love, God's outrageous love, results in our becoming little because we can't act and we can't be otherwise.

Something inside me used to rebel when I was told that we don't amount to much or that we are good for nothing. Deep down, I know I'm precious in God's sight and in the eyes of others as well. I'm worth something, and I refuse to say I'm nothing. I should say, I used to refuse. Because all of a sudden and deep inside, I understand perfectly that being little isn't something negative. It's not a way of diminishing oneself, making oneself small so that somebody else can have more room. No, Jesus already has a lot of room, and all I have is a little bit of room. But the little bit of room I have is marvelous. I'm not put down, diminished. I'm simply overcome by the love that I feel in this moment, and I can only declare that he inhabits everything, includes everything, penetrates everything.

So I'm not going to try to compete. In the face of so much, I yield with joy.

> I really do want to be little in this way, Lord. I really do, because when I do, I feel like a queen.

> ☩ *Nicole, if you knew just how intense my love is, you would be paralyzed. You would not be able to move.*

> I believe you, Jesus. I believe you.

It really is from the inside that he allows me to enter into his kingdom. It's mad. I begin to cry. It's stronger than I am.

September 25

Gather me into yourself, Lord, because I'm not managing to place myself in your presence.

✝ *I will gather you.*

I feel hopelessly scattered. My mind doesn't obey me and goes wandering off in all directions. This evening's dinner, Laurette's homework, tomorrow's shopping . . . If I keep on this way, he will not come. So I try as hard as I can to quiet down. At the Consecration I'm finally more ready to receive him.

It would be stupid to miss a meeting with you, Lord.

He doesn't reply.

After the Consecration, I finally have some peace and quiet.

Thank you.

✝ *Keep your eyes wide open to the world, to the events and people that I place in your life. But keep your eyes closed when you are on the way. I will lead you on the way. Do not worry. Be like a child and let yourself be led.*

I need to look inward, to listen to his word, and to follow his road.

September 26

Ever since this morning, the idea has been running through my head that the Lord is a "marginal." As I'm doing house-work and preparing lunch, I wonder if it comes from him or from me. I'll wait. Maybe this evening at Mass.

Mass at the Hermitage.

The Gospel: "Who do you say that I am?"

You're the "marginal," Jesus? Is that it?

✝ *Yes.*

Explain that a bit. Does it mean you're out on the fringe?

✝ *Yes. Do not try to close me up in a system or file me in a drawer. I will spill out of the drawer. Do not try to contain me, to bring me down to size. If you do that, I will escape from you. Do you understand?*

Yes, I understand; but then how do we reach you, learn from you, meet you?

✝ *Heart to heart, Nicole.*

Yes, I think I know that. Is there any other way?

✝ *No.*

Well then, what a responsibility, this dialogue, this heart-to-heart talk with you. What an opportunity! But looking at it this way is a little scary, Jesus.

✝ *Do not worry, Nicole. We are two. I am inviting you. I myself am inviting you.*

September 27

✝ *I invite you. It is I who invite you.*

September 28

A hectic day. We are beleaguered by telephone calls, errands, and a trip to the Hermitage and back. Pierre seems drained this evening. My heart aches as I see him sitting at the table in the chapel. There are three of us.

After the Consecration the Lord says to me:

> ✝ *Come and dance with me, Nicole. Come.*

This is too much! Too much! I feel a few moments of panic as I hear a little voice inside me say, *You're wrong. Your imagination is playing tricks on you. . . .*

I burrow down into the silence.

> Come and help me, Lord. Is it you who are speaking to me?
>
> ✝ *Come and dance with me. Come. I am inviting you. Do not leave me by myself.*

At that I explode:

> Look here, Lord. You're going too far. Don't you think this is a bit much? The world is a mess, Pierre is physically exhausted, the Companion next to him tonight isn't any better. And you're asking me to dance with you?

I'm screaming inside.

✝ *Yes. Come.*

A few minutes of silence pass. He's sad.

✝ *Come. Do not leave me by myself. I am not asking you to come and dance with the world, but with me.*

You want me to come and enjoy being with you?

✝ *Yes.*

And all the rest, all the others? All that comes later?

✝ *Yes.*

That's how Jesus inwardly leads me to discover praise and joy. This is really crazy.

September 29

Always this nagging fear that he won't come. There are
four of us this evening. During Mass, before the
Consecration, he speaks to me gently, as if to reassure me.

✢ *I am like a raincoat.*

What a strange notion, Lord.

But I wait. If this is really from him, he will explain it to me.

After the Consecration:

✢ *You put me on like a raincoat.*

Go on.

✢ *I am the raincoat. You feel me. The lining is
pleasant to the touch. The storms, the wind,
the rain will come and drench the raincoat,
but not you. Do you understand? I protect
you.*

The wind, the storms, the rain . . . all these are
our human and material difficulties?

✢ *Yes. I do not take them away. I protect you.
First, live in me.*

September 30

Gospel: Luke, the end of chapter 9.

I'm following you, Jesus. We are following you. But the plow is hard to manage.

✢ *You are mistaken.*

Really? . . .

✢ *Yes, you are mistaken. I am the one who opens the furrow, who moves ahead. The plow is me.*

What about me? What about us? The plow can't go forward all by itself.

✢ *Take hold of it. Grasp it with both hands. If you hold it steady and do your best to guide it, I will do the rest.*

October 3

I have just made the rounds of the farm. The Companions are working. There is a kind of peacefulness. And yet these are broken men. I stop in the chapel for a few moments.

Thank you for this peace, Lord. Every time I come out here, I'm just amazed how well these men are able to live together.

✝ *They are the image of what you are for me.*

Do you mean that sometimes, like them, we are miserable and unfaithful, and then, at other times, we are gentle and obedient?

✝ *Yes. Treat them as I treat you. Be patient, watchful. If they decide to leave you, to aban-don what you hold out to them, love them in spite of everything. Even from afar, continue to love them.*

Yes, I understand.

And then, after a moment of silence:

Lord, is it pride if I say that I'm not like them? Am I being proud? Tell me.

✠ *You are different, because I dwell in you, I
live in you. You are rich because of me.*

As I leave the chapel, I realize that the Lord didn't exactly answer my question. I'll ask him about it tomorrow, or the day after. Later.

October 5

I speak to him at the beginning of the Mass.

> Are you going to answer me, Lord? Clarify
> some things for me?
>
> ✝ *Yes. Wait.*

I wait. The Gospel reminds us that we are worthless
servants.

> Worthless? That "worthless" irritates me. Is it
> pride?
>
> ✝ *Be like a leaf in the wind, the cold and dry*
> *north wind. In autumn the leaf lets itself be*
> *carried wherever the breeze takes it. Do you*
> *understand?*
>
> Yes, I think so. You are the wind, and you want
> me to hand myself over to you completely.
>
> ✝ *Yes.*

And then, once again, everything becomes clear to me.

> My pride consists in not accepting your love
> simply and totally. That's the way I see it.
>
> ✝ *Yes, Nicole, yes.*

You really do want me to be like a leaf?

✝ *Yes.*

And just like that I'll become worthless, but it doesn't matter. Is that what you're trying to tell me?

✝ *Yes. What is important is the wind, the immensity of my love.*

What Jesus offers us is an abyss, and in this abyss there is only life to the full. But all I can do is hem and haw and protest that it's too good to be true.

At the end of Mass I ask his pardon:

> You talk to me, you give me proof upon proof of your love, and still I hesitate.

He smiles. He seems happy to have cleared things up for me.

On my way home I tell myself that Jesus really has chosen me. Someday I'll be able to tell him in all sincerity: Do with me what you will. I'm going to try; I'm going to make a start. But it makes my head swim.

> I'm going to try. Both of us are going to try, Lord.

October 6

The Lord comes and invites me and the rest of us to dance.

Is it because I like dancing so much that you're
inviting me again?

✝ *Yes.*

He smiles. I let myself be led by him, and I'm happy, profoundly happy.

Do you have something to say to me?

✝ *Yes. Remove the useless garments you cover
me with.*

We continue to dance. He really did invite me.

Just what do you mean?

✝ *I am neither a moralist nor a philosopher. Rid
me of all that. My only garment is tenderness
and mercy. Do you understand?*

Is that why you invite me to dance with you?

✝ *Yes. I want you to feel this tenderness.*

You know, I'm so happy when I'm with you that I want it to last.

He smiles.

✝ *Do not worry.*

October 7

And the dance goes on. We continue to dance, and Mary looks at us, smiling.

Dance with my Son. It makes me happy.

We go faster. We really are dancing! Mary is happy, and so am I, because I love to dance.

Mary says:

If your head starts spinning as you're whirling around, hold on to him. He will steady you. You won't fall.

On the inside, I really am dancing with him.

October 8

I have just been at a dinner with the volunteers who help with the sale of used goods. I'm a little down. Since they're not part of the Community, they don't always take our point of view into consideration. When I say *our,* I mean Pierre and me and all that we're trying to do. I know this is inevitable even though there is goodwill on both sides.

Lord, it's stupid to get upset over such little things. We're all walking toward you and working for you. Why aren't we more united?

✝ *Nicole, is my invisible kingdom being woven?*

Yes.

✝ *Well then?*

But why don't we have the unity and harmony that I can feel with others: Bernard, Jean-Claude, Pierre, Dominique . . .

✝ *Once again, you are mistaken. I am the unity and harmony you seek. If you want to find it, do not look anywhere else but in me.*

But, Lord, what about those I have just mentioned?

✝ *They live in me, and you also live in me. Do you understand?*

Yes.

The Lord is stubborn. He really wants me to dance with him.

October 8

There are two of us. In a true spirit of harmony.

Do you really want me to follow you as if you were living?

✝ *Yes. I am alive.*

Where do you want to take me?

✝ *That is not your concern. Follow me.*

All right.

October 10

MASS AT THE HERMITAGE

✣ *Follow me. Follow me. Come and dance with me.*

You really are determined to seduce us, Lord.

✣ *I can deceive your body, and I can deceive your mind, but I cannot deceive your heart. Come and dance with me, heart to heart.*

October 11

I'm doing the ironing and the results are hardly impeccable. In a way, my ironing is an image of what I know how to do, which is to say, I don't know how to do anything very well. I take that back. When I think about it, it seems to me that I do know how to do two things well: teach or give talks and knit. The rest falls pretty short. And still the Lord comes to speak to me, to dwell in me, and to lead me into the unknown. It doesn't make any sense. I tell him so.

> Why me? Why are you weaving this adventure between the two of us? Why? Why? Tell me.

> ☩ *Because I have chosen you. Because I need you.*

> To go where?

> ☩ *Into the unknown. There you have it. Do you accept?*

In the laundry as I continue my so-so job of ironing, I let these words sink into me.

I really should be afraid; at least some part of me should be afraid. Suddenly I feel close to those who betrayed Jesus. Often, very often—in fact, ever since I was a child—I have wondered why the disciples of Jesus who saw his miracles, who lived with him, who saw him walk on the water and multiply the loaves, were so thickheaded, so hard-hearted. All these proofs took place right in front of their eyes, and yet . . . Jesus has given me the incredible gift of speaking to me, of making me grow. And yet, in spite of all these proofs, I quibble. . . .

✝ *Come and follow me.*

I'll try. But you're going to have to help me. A lot.

✝ *I will.*

October 12

A telephone call this morning. Pierre informs me that a Companion has just tried to commit suicide. They're trying to revive him at the hospital. I'm not completely surprised. We talked yesterday, and in the afternoon especially, when he phoned me, he sounded so miserable that I suggested that he return to the Hermitage. He did. We weren't there, and he swallowed a bottle of pills.

Philippe consoles me, telling me that this is no time for what-ifs.

Later, in spite of the sadness I feel—or, rather, along with it—a sense of peace comes over me. I didn't ask for it. It's simply given. This evening at Mass there is still no news of the Companion. I speak to the Lord:

> It's you who give me this peace, Lord.

> ✚ *Yes. I am the raincoat. Come and dance with me.*

> This is almost scandalous, Lord. You ask me to dance with you while a Companion is in the hospital.

> ✚ *Come and dance.*

I have my head in my hands, and at the same time I feel some force drawing my face upward with great tenderness. I can't resist. I am happy.

Why, Lord? Why this peace?

✝ *I come first, and then the Companion.*

October 16

A getaway with Philippe for several days.

I alight on another planet, totally different from that of the Companions. Once again I feel very much the stranger.

I often distance myself from the group to be alone and to enjoy the sea and the sky.

We speak to each other.

> Lord, now that I have these incredible conversations with you, why don't you come and sit alongside me. Why don't you just stay with me a little?

> ✝ *Later, Nicole. Later, in my eternity.*

I don't give up:

> But why not now? You know that I'd really like to have you stay at my side. I love the way you speak to me. So you could also stay with me and tell me where you're taking me, what you want of me. Then it would be clear, and I'd go.

> ✝ *No.*

Why not?

✝ *I am not an officer, nor are you a soldier. I will not give you orders.*

I'd almost prefer that you did.

✝ *I know.*

I let these words sink deeply into me.

It's really a relationship that you want. That's the whole thing.

✝ *Nicole, I am alive.*

October 20

Back with the Companions again. All sorts of little problems and tensions. Another suicide attempt, and here I am once again in the middle of this "bazaar," where everything happens so fast. Pierre is exhausted, but still smiling. There are thirty of us, and besides that, during the day Pierre takes care of the street people, giving them a meal in exchange for a little work around the place.

I feel faint.

We are going to go under, Lord.

✝ *No.*

Later at Mass, after the Eucharist. An image of a slope in the mountains. The Lord is walking in front of us.

You look like Philippe, Lord.

✝ *Yes.*

In the mountains, walking behind Philippe, I know that nothing will happen to me. He's a lot stronger than I am, and his slow, sure-footed stride gives me confidence.

What is it you want me to understand?

✝ *I am clearing the way so that it will not be so difficult for you. Let me go well in front of you.*

If it becomes too difficult, will you hoist me up?

✝ *Yes.*

October 21

We are back at the chapel with Pierre. We have to have a down-to-earth conversation with one of the staff who isn't doing his job and who is proving to be a destructive element in the Community.

Pierre prays. I speak to the Lord.

> Lord, what we are about to do isn't easy.

> ✝ *Yes, I know.*

In some part of me I feel at peace. But I also feel tension and uneasiness. That weighs me down.

> ✝ *I am not going to take away the uneasiness and the difficulty, Nicole. Bring my peace to it. Let me walk in front of you.*

> All right, Lord.

Pierre opens the Bible to two texts about false prophets. Now we are armed for battle.

I feel my heart beating even before I open my mouth during the interview. I say what I have to say as the person responsible for the Community. I'm firm and decisive. I have to be. But at the same time I have compassion for this man who hasn't been on the up-and-up with us and who criticizes us behind our backs.

Everything goes well, or at least as well as can be expected. The falsehood has been unmasked and a certain level of peace has been restored.

The Lord helped me by keeping me from becoming mean and settling my own accounts. Humanly speaking, it would have been perfectly within my right to do so. But since I put his interests ahead of my own, Jesus gave me compassion instead. I had nothing to do with it. It was Jesus.

There will be other difficult times, I'm sure of it. But tonight at Mass I thank the Lord. There is a song in my heart.

A prayer meeting with a group of sisters. In general, the Lord is really spoiling me, and the Spirit breathes by making use of me. This evening the image is that of a stairway with steps.

I speak to him:

> Lord, I'm exhausted and empty this evening.
> Moreover, the image I have this evening must
> come from me because it's really what Pierre
> and I have gone through today.

> ✝ *Tell them about it, Nicole.*

> Do you really want me to tell them?

> ✝ *Yes.*

I hesitate a little, because this evening I really would prefer to be carried along by the others, to let Pierre take the lead and simply follow along.

✢ *Tell them about it.*

I speak. I tell them we don't have to worry about the whole stairway, just single steps. When it's necessary, Jesus will wait on a step with us, help us get up on the next one, hoist us up to the third. Our business, our job, is the step. The Lord takes care of the entire stairway. We each have our own part to play.

A little flower from the Lord at the close of the prayer meeting: the sisters attest that it really is the Spirit who spoke through this image.

An elderly sister, on leaving, takes my hand and, holding it in hers, says to me like a mother superior:

Don't be troubled. It's the Spirit who is speaking through you.

October 23

Great repose. I feel very relaxed, and I have the impression of letting myself sink into a luminous black ocean. It's peaceful, and I feel very much present, but also drowsy. I seem to be very, very far away, and yet very much with the people who are participating in the Eucharist. When it comes time for the sign of peace, I'm so buried in the Lord that I can hardly lift my head. Pierre appears transformed, like someone else. His face is the same because I recognize him, and yet he looks completely different. I'm not bothered by it; quite the contrary. It's a little as if his face were washed clean of every human trace, becoming more luminous and less clearly delineated. Is this the way we will look in eternity? Maybe.

> Thank you for giving me a taste of all this,
> Jesus. Thank you.

Later:

> You're giving me strength. I have the impression
> that we are going to need it. Thank you.

All Saints' Week

In the car that takes me and seven kids to Batz-sur-Mer, I thank the Lord for this week of rest ahead of us and for the little voices chattering behind me. I'm spoiled. The Lord gives me an image, a peculiar image. It's of a container filled to overflowing with mousse, as if someone had overdone the recipe.

Tell me why you have given me such a peculiar image, Lord.

✝ *I am the mousse. If you bury yourself in me, I will overflow without your having to do anything. Do not do anything. Let go.*

October 28 and 29

I meditate on the image of the overflowing mousse.

> You know, Lord, it's hard for me to accept this "Do not do anything." I feel like I'm thousands of miles away from you. This immense love of yours that I feel today is boundless. How can your omnipotence need my collaboration? You, the All-Powerful; me, not only little, but in a certain sense nothing at all. And there you are, asking me to make the mousse together with you! You have to admit that this isn't just unseemly. It's preposterous!

> ✝ *Yes, I know.*

> You seem a little sad.

> ✝ *Yes.*

A few moments later:

> Do you know what, Lord? I really think there's something impossible about the route you propose for your friends. It's not so surprising that more don't follow you.

> ✝ *My words have been distorted, Nicole. I already told you that.*

You know, on the inside I'm beginning to understand your secret. It's all about heart-to-heart.
But it's so unsettling. I have the impression that
I'm like an onion, and you're taking away layer
after layer. What will be left?

✝ *You. At any rate, each time I take a layer
away, I clothe you again with my cloak.*

I reflect on what he has said. It's true. I'd be untrue to
myself if I thought otherwise. Every time I was afraid and
gave this fear to the Lord in order to find peace again, he
gave me peace.

And you, Lord, you gave me Bernard to trust in me when I
was ready to give up. You gave me Cécile's smile and her
helping hand when I felt so bad for her. All those for whom
and with whom I suffered are with you and me, as if we
were welded together. It's true.

And later:

What do you want me to do?

✝ *Intercede.*

As Thérèse told me to do?

✝ *Yes.*

And, in fact, at night, before I go to sleep or when I wake
up in the night, I entrust the prayer intentions that people
have given me to the Lord.

Do not worry, Jesus. I'm going to try.

November 1

Mass at the church.

Our number rose to fifteen two days ago, and this evening, without any argument or bickering, we headed off to church.

The children are here with their friends. They're all different, and some of them hardly ever go to Mass, but they're here. My heart is filled with joy during the Mass. Martine, a friend of mine, is next to me. We don't talk, but I know that the three of us are united.

> Thank you for Martine, for the children, for this vacation.

There is something touching about this odd little group. These days have been marked by a heightened sense of peace and joy.

It's hard to forget the young people—or the grown-ups—who are sitting in the two pews behind us. I can hardly keep from laughing when Benoît, who is taking up the collection, makes a scene and accuses me out loud of putting "Turkish" money in the collection basket. (Some Tunisian coins did get into my purse by mistake.)

After Communion I try to draw closer to Jesus and to be silent. It's a little tough to do.

✝ *I will do wondrous things through you.*

A few moments later:

Are you going to tell me once again to let go?

✝ *Yes.*

A little later:

✝ *Let go. Be light, like a seagull.*

Light?

✝ *Yes, light. Do not weigh others down, and do not try to control them too much. Be light, not indifferent, but light.*

Why?

✝ *Because the lightness allows me to come through. I will take charge. I will do the carrying. Your lightness will point to me, unveil me.*

The Lord comes and sits down next to us.

✝ *Hold on to my hand.*

A little later I have the image of two hands intertwined. The image is strong. Is it something I have dreamed up? I wait. The confirmation comes from Pierre. "Thank you for being in love with us," he says. After the Consecration, Jesus clarifies its meaning for us:

✝ *Walk with me. Go forward. Let us go forward like lovers.*

Please go on. Explain it further.

✝ *Carefree, both of us as lighthearted as lovers.*

Today it's difficult, almost painful, for me to immerse myself in the Lord.

I feel far away from you, Lord.

Silence.

Such mediocrity today, Lord.

☩ *Give it to me.*

Take it, Lord. It seems that this is all I have to offer today. It's pretty wretched, isn't it?

I feel unhappy and really miserable.

Then, at the very moment that I say these words, I'm invaded by a heavy, brutal peace. I feel myself drawn down to the ground. Around me I hear voices giving thanks for this word. Praise ascends from their hearts while I bury myself in a kind of thick cloud. I seem to be between two worlds. My heart is warmed by the praise.

Listen, Lord, receive it. They're crying to you.

I'm all by myself. And so we talk—or, rather, I talk and he listens. My words to him today are terribly commonplace, little more than "thank you" and "I love you."

Before arriving at the farm I pass in front of a wooded area. The colors are magnificent, varied, and resplendent. I have the impression that I'm seeing them for the first time.

   ✝ *It is like my kingdom, Nicole.*

Your kingdom?

   ✝ *My invisible kingdom. You are just beginning to discover it. It will be just as beautiful and varied.*

November 7

Philippe and Thierry have just left me. I carry their two beautiful smiles with me onto the train platform.

Cardinal Gantin invited me to come to Rome after he had read the little notebook. He's part of the family because my grandmother paid for his studies when he was young. When I was making a miniretreat at Saint-Benoît, I got the idea to send my little notebook to one of the pope's right-hand men.

"Go ahead," my Uncle Pierre, a monk at Saint-Benoît, said to me. "That's not a bad idea at all."

On the very day of my birthday, Cardinal Gantin called from Rome to say he would like to meet me. It was ten o'clock in the evening, and it was hard for me to understand him because the connection was so poor. At one point I thought he was one of the Companions and almost got angry with him!

Several days later, at the Apostolic Nunciature in Paris, I met him and discovered this great man of God. I was struck by his sharp intelligence, the way he listened, his love for Mary, and, above all, his humility. I had been afraid that I was going to meet an ecclesiastical dignitary who would advise me to take care of my children and my husband and to be careful about a certain kind of mysticism. On the contrary, I met a brother. He was attentive, gentle, happy to listen to me. In no time we were at the heart of the matter: Mary, the pope, the importance of marriage, and the question that was most central for me:

"How do you manage to hold the two together?"

Sensing my incomprehension, Cardinal Gantin explains, "How do you hold together the violent world of the Companions and the world of your family?"

I tell him. He listens with eyes closed and he understands. He understands everything: what is at stake in keeping a balance, the squabbles, my enthusiasm about continuing because, with Pierre and prayer, I'm armed.

"Continue," he tells me. "Like the pope, you are not afraid. Continue."

The hour passes. I have to be on my way. He gives me back my treasure.

"Come to Rome. I'd like the pope to give you his personal blessing. Come whenever you would like."

And so here I am on the train for Rome. I didn't plan this. I didn't ask for anything. In my head ring the words of the Lord, "I will make you a queen." And at the same time I remember Pierre's advice: "Little servant. Always be a little servant." Both at one and the same time. My head and heart are filled with those who have led me to this joy. My grandmother; my father, who, on a day when I experienced a great setback, told me to pray to Mary; Uncle Paul; Uncle André; Uncle Pierre; and now Bernard and Pierre.

What beacons! How tightly we are bound together! All of you are very much alive and present in my heart, and I'll make time to pray with you and for you.

November 9

I have been invited to Mass in Cardinal Gantin's private chapel. There are three of us. It's very simple. Even though I'm in a palace that houses several cardinals, even though I'm far away from the open skies of the Beauce, this chapel is so much like ours that I feel at home. It's small and simple. It's the same family that comes before the Lord.

Cardinal Gantin treats me with the kindness and gentleness one would show to a younger sister. It's a shame he's so terribly busy, because I would like to spend more time with him. But I don't want to add to his burdens, so I drink my tea and take my leave.

Before going to sleep I thank the Lord for spoiling me like this. I confide to his care this older brother with whom I have been able to share prayer and daily life so deeply.

The next day, Jesus says to me:

✝ *Stay small.*

Yes, Lord, but you know, I may not be able to keep myself from being proud!

✝ *Little, Nicole, little.*

I have you, the Son of God, for my friend. I
carry within myself all those you have given me.
And the day after tomorrow I'm going to see the
pope. How can I help being proud?

✞ *Proud, but little.*

Why are you so insistent?

✞ *So that you will let me walk well in front of*
you.

November 10

I'm going to see the pope. . . . I'm going to see the pope.

That silly little refrain keeps going through my head, taking me back to the times in my childhood when I'd feel like singing a little tune over and over again and dancing to it.

I seem to have become a little girl again, and yet . . . and yet, I feel that there is something that isn't quite right between me and Jesus.

As I go from church to church, I often stop to pray, of course. Each time it seems as if Jesus were repeating the same words to me: "Be little."

It's become almost an obsession. In the crowded bus I'm riding, I say to him:

> You're so insistent that it makes me feel uneasy.

He doesn't reply.

So I insist:

> What is it, Jesus? You seem to be sad. Tell me why.

> ✝ *Take me along.*

What? That's a bit strong. It's your home I'm going to.

✝ *I do not have a home. Take me with you.*

I'm nonplused. Silence.

Do you feel hurt?

✝ *Yes.*

I want to argue with him, to assure him of my good faith, and then suddenly I realize that it would be useless.

In completely good faith, I had quite simply forgotten about him. Like a little child following behind you, he had to remind me he was there. It's all topsy-turvy. I'm the one who is taking Jesus with me to see the pope!

I'm totally confused. I wait until I'm calm again before I promise him:

I'll take you with me. I promise.

November 12

I promised, and so I do it. He's at my side as we enter the audience hall.

Thanks to Cardinal Gantin, I was in the first row and could see the pope close up. The presence and power of this man are awesome.

Lord, watch over him, clothe him, dwell in him.

That was practically my only prayer.

When Pope John Paul approached me and looked at me for a few seconds before blessing me, what I saw was the look of a man who has been, who is being, crucified. Yes, this man has already been crucified. I was literally swallowed up by his gaze, a look so deep it seemed to come from some faraway place and to be filled with a tenderness that was forceful and direct.

Carry on, Holy Father. Even though you may be all alone and everyone is against you, carry on.

There is such solitude about this man.

I prayed for this man, John Paul II, asking Jesus to come and dwell in his solitude.

November 13

A day of shopping in Rome.

Yesterday's joy fills my day.

November 14

Last night and all day today were tumultuous. I feel as if I'd been in a knock-down, drag-out fight. There's no other way to describe it.

Every morning now I have been getting up early in order to go to Mass. Up until now I always experienced the same feeling of joy that I feel when I go to Mass at the Companions. But this morning I was overtaken by a feeling of heaviness. There is no reason for it. During the Mass I know the joy of the encounter, but at the same time I feel such a heavy weight that tears stream from my eyes. I can't do anything to stop them, these tears of sadness. The feeling lasts all morning long, and I have to ask myself some questions. This isn't normal because there is absolutely no reason to be sad. Quite the contrary. Everything makes me happy for one reason or another: all that I'm experiencing here, the people I carry in my heart, the freedom of time and space that has been afforded me. And yet . . .

Exhausted from struggling against tears whose origin I don't know but which I can hardly contain in the presence of others, I retire to my room and let them flow. They pour out. I feel completely despondent.

I'm going to try to rest and get some sleep, but before I do that, I speak to him.

> Lord, I don't understand anything, and that makes it so hard. If I knew why, or perhaps if I knew what to call this unknown depression, I could deal with it. But I don't know.

No reply.

> All right. I place my heart next to yours. Protect me, because I'm weak and ignorant. If it's the Evil One who has been troubling me, protect me.

I cry myself to sleep.

I wake up an hour later. The tempest has passed. I feel lighter.

After calmly taking the time to write some letters and cards, I go down to the chapel.

> It's better now, Lord. But I really don't understand what happened to me.

> ✝ *You have passed through a little bit of the night; you have carried a part of my cross.*

Is it you, you, Jesus, who are sending me this?

> ✝ *Nicole, Nicole . . .*

But put yourself in my place.

> ✝ *Nicole, I am shaping you. You have to know, have to experience this part of my kingdom, too.*

I allow these words to sink in. This is something new. It's not easy, and I try my best to discern if it's he or my imagination.

Finally I'm able to smile. The little lamp burning next to the tabernacle warms me.

I'll follow you, Lord. I'll follow you.

✝ *It was not so difficult after all, so heavy. Do you not see how near I am?*

A little touch of humor on the Lord's part.

November 19

It's not easy to place myself in the Lord's presence once again. My head is swimming with images and impressions of Rome and especially of the strength I had the good fortune to draw on. I feel it inside me. It's something that wells up and abides in me.

> Lord, I feel distant and empty, a bit like a foreigner. I don't feel ready. Come.

Silence. Jesus isn't bullied. I can't summon him. There is no call button. He is, and he is gentle, and I flounder around, but I know he's here and very much alive.

> Still, come and speak to me. You know how much I need to hear you. Come.

Silence.

After the Consecration:

> ✝ *Make some room for me. Your house is too full.*

What do you mean?

> ✝ *There is too much furniture in the room set aside for me.*

When you say room, do you mean our hearts?

✝ *Yes.*

What do you want us to do?

✝ *Remove what is not absolutely necessary.*
Then I will be more comfortable being with
you. Give me lots of space.

Remove? All right, but what?

✝ *Your cares, your useless worrying. Do not*
weigh yourself down.

It's not all that easy to put our cares aside. I try. A little
later:

✝ *Nicole, I was born in a stable.*

In a stable! . . .

November 20

For the past couple of days I have been questioning myself and meditating on detachment. Cardinal Gantin spoke about it during one of the Masses in his little chapel, and ever since then I have been thinking about it. I find it disconcerting.

Today, as I'm walking to the Secours Catholique, he clarifies what it means.

✝ *Once again, Nicole, it's not something negative.*

You're right. Once again I was under the impression that it was something negative, that to detach oneself is in some way to love less. But the fact is you give me people to love and who love me.

✝ *Be like the pope.*

What? . . . The pope?

✝ *Yes. He has his arms wide open. Be like him.*

That's detachment?

✝ *Yes.*

What do you mean?

✝ *Love, Nicole, love all those I give you. Love. But do not hold them too tight, not one of them alone or all of them.*

Why not?

✝ *If you did, I would not be able to give you anyone else. You would not leave me enough room.*

I understand. Do you have anything else to tell me?

✝ *Yes. If you do this, I will love in you.*

How will you manage that?

✝ *I will inscribe them in your heart. I will love them in you. Not only will I not take them away, but I will inscribe them in you. Do you understand?*

Yes.

Oh yes, not only do I understand, but I have been reassured and given a sign of appreciation: "I will inscribe them in you."

Who am I that Jesus should come and do this in me? Who am I? I am literally flooded with joy. I feel like crying, like shouting thank you, but all I can do is say to him in a low voice:

Thank you. Thank you. Go ahead. Inscribe them in me.

"Abandon yourself," the Cardinal told me. I went away carrying these two words as a child carries her treasures.

And at this very moment, I abandon myself.

November 22

The sweetness of Jesus caressing my cheek after the Eucharist.

✢ *Do not make any plans. I will take care of everything.*

November 23

The Apocalypse of St. John.

Pierre emphasizes that we are chosen. I'm bothered by the word *irreproachable.*

> Lord, you have chosen us, but I'm far from being irreproachable.

After the Consecration, he gives an explanation:

> ✢ *The woman of the Gospel, the one who gives what is essential. Be like her.*

I meditate on this, but I don't get the connection with the word *irreproachable.*

> You want me to give what is essential. You really want the essence of who I am?

> ✢ *Yes, everything. The good and the not-so-good. Everything.*

> As to the good, Lord, you know that I'm not stupid, that I've done advanced studies and I'm a good prof. Sometimes it's a little difficult to give all that up to take care of thirty guys who come in off the street. Is that the essential that you want?

✝ *Yes. Your gifts, your intelligence, but also your limitations and your deficiencies. Give me all of it.*

Jesus, you know that I don't do too badly with the talents you've given me.

✝ *I will do even better than you. Do you not believe that I will be able to do at least as well as you?*

Of course. But what about the part that's not so good, the limitations, the deficiencies?

✝ *There I will do what you are not able to do.*

You have an answer for everything. You always corner me.

✝ *No, I do not corner you; I set you on course.*

The Lord isn't any more distant from me, but he shows himself in a different way.

✝ *I am building a wall to protect you. I myself
am this wall, within you and around you.*

December 8

✝ *Take me now as your protector. From the very depths of your being.*

December 9

It's hard for me to place myself in the presence of the Lord.
A little later, I speak to the Lord.

> Make use of me if you need me.

I try to make myself little. Several words rise up in me.

Jesus says:

> ✝ *Let go. Tell them that.*

I don't remember all the words because they didn't come
from me. I have a very strong impression that the Lord is
speaking to one or the other of the sisters. It's as if I were
only a conduit. I feel something inside pushing me to say:

> Go, go to your brothers. Don't try to avoid it. I
> have put you where you belong.

I feel in my body that these words are meant for someone
in the group. I don't try to find out who. That's the Lord's
business, not mine.

A little later another phrase comes to me:

> ✝ *Unarmed, vulnerable, little. That is the way*
> *you must go to your brothers. Like me,*
> *unarmed, vulnerable, little.*

December 10

I have to admit that I'm a little disappointed that I no longer experience the deep interiority of the conversations of the previous months.

Lord, don't abandon me. I need to hear you.

✝ *I have already said so much to you, Nicole.*
Live what I have helped you discover.

But I'm afraid.

✝ *Yes, I know. I can see that.*

Later:

✝ *Do you really think that I could deceive you?*
Do not be afraid. Do not doubt.

December 11

✠ *Be lighthearted, carefree.*

That's a little hard right now, Lord.

✠ *I want you to be lighthearted. I want all of you to come to me like little children and throw your arms around me. I will carry you.*

December 11

✝ *Be little; abandon yourself.*

I'm trying to.

✝ *I am going to use you like a conduit. Do not get in the way.*

I'm afraid. What we have to live through is so insane.

✝ *Do not get in the way. Do not be afraid.*

Later he asks me to say:

✝ *Do not be afraid. Do not try to make all sorts of preparations for what lies ahead, for tomorrow. I will give you the strength you need when you need it.*

End of December

The days fly by fast and full. As Christmas draws near I always feel a special kind of joy. This joy is given to me every year, and I'm happy to go running here and there in search of something that will delight this person or that person.

I feel the Lord is watching over me.

Those remarkable moments of intimacy with the Lord haven't disappeared, but they seem to have changed somewhat. During the Eucharist the Lord is close by, certainly, but now I no longer experience moments in which time and space are momentarily suspended. I have to admit that I miss these intense moments, but I'm trying not to make them up or will them. There is a deep-down sense of well-being in feeling myself surrounded by the tenderness of God without losing anything of my own personality. It's as if everything I'm searching for, consciously or not, were being realized. What was so fantastic about those moments I experienced was feeling that I was in the arms of Jesus and at the same time closer than ever to those I love. I don't remove myself from them. They're with me naturally.

And so how could I not want more of this?

It's when you want, isn't it? I was told to abandon myself. Pierre often reminds me to be little. So I try.

A day trip to Paray-le-Monial in response to a request from the Sisters of the Cenacle to speak about our involvement with the poor. What a joy it was to see Genviève's smile again. I spoke to the sisters about the way Jesus takes care of me, of us. I tried to be as sincere and straightforward as possible. Even without trying to be someone I'm not, I find that it's not easy to speak about our life. I have the impression that every time I try to speak or explain what it's all about, I monopolize Jesus or make him into something he isn't. I try to avoid this kind of distortion by talking from my own life experience. Those who hear me, like those who might happen to read this notebook, will know what comes from me and what comes from him.

✝ *Do not strain. With simplicity accept all that I
give you to live. Do not force anything. I will
take care of the rest.*

Christmas

Whenever I'm in the midst of a gathering that is somewhat agitated and unfamiliar, it's difficult to allow the Lord to enter deeply within me. I tell him so.

It's difficult, you know, to let go, to come back to you.

✝ *Yes, I know that.*

I sense his presence. He's here, alive. He's something like an older brother who wants to let me walk all by myself, but who also wants to protect me. He watches over me. At the Consecration I'm able to say to him in all truth:

Do with me whatever you wish. I'll be your follower.

I say this with my whole being: head, heart, body.

A little later:

Lord, I'm being completely honest. You know I am. It wasn't some rush of sentimentality that led me to say what I just said. . . . But I'm not stronger than St. Peter, you know. You will have to help me if I should ever leave you.

✝ *Do not worry. I will come after you and take you by the sleeve.*

Christmas Day

The Companions are here, around the table. Pierre is with them. Peace reigns, but hardly anyone speaks. This is a Christmas without wife, without children, without family. I'm absolutely certain that the child who was born in a stable and died on a cross is one of theirs and that he came for them.

> Lord, I beg you to send out harvesters. Send more Pierres, Bernards, Jean-Claudes. Send even more, if such should be your pleasure.

After Christmas

The rhythm of my life has become rather hectic and broken. The children are on vacation. I have the flu. And then Philippe comes down with it, too. I'm exhausted and have a hard time keeping up. Not feeling the presence of the Lord as strongly as I did a year ago makes me a little sad.

I know that he's here, especially during the Eucharist. I have promised to be little and to abandon myself. So I'll try not to be so sad.

I have the impression that I'm living through a kind of intermission, both in my soul and also at the Companions. We're letting go.

January 10

Once again I'm in the presence of the Lord. Pierre, a Companion, Bernadette, and I.

I come before him once again and say:

> As you wish, when you wish. I'm not asking for anything.

A few moments later I'm literally plunged into his presence. It's interminably long and deep. Now I am reassured.

I hear:

> ✝ *Little girl, little girl . . . little sister, little sister.*

The words overwhelm me with their tenderness and love. Later I have an image of the Lord walking in front of me like an older brother while I'm running behind him, trying to catch up.

> ✝ *Do not be so frantic. Why are you running like that?*

In order to catch up with you.

> ✝ *Do not be worried. I will watch over you like an older brother. I will wait for you. Do not run so fast. Do not force things.*

January 11

I am here in your presence. I'm little, as you want me to be.

✝ *Do not worry.*

After Communion:

✝ *I am the light. It travels through thick layers of darkness to get to you. You only receive a part of it. That is enough.*

The image is very clear to me. It's like the light of a very strong projector that has to cut through thick layers of darkness in order finally to get to us.

Why all these thick layers, Lord?

✝ *I will tell you tomorrow.*

January 12

It's so cold in the chapel that we have to take refuge in Pierre's office.

Pierre is worn out, empty. He's been listening to a friend who arrived from abroad and never stopped talking. Pierre is smiling, but I see profound weariness on his face.

It's time for Mass. Finally we are going to be able to rest with him.

> Lord, there is sorrow in my heart because of
> Pierre, but here I am, here we all are in your
> presence. I feel tired, on edge, and short of
> energy this evening. Come.

I try to submerge myself in his presence and in the rest he offers us.

After Communion:

> What are these thick layers, Lord? You told me
> you'd say something about that.

> ✝ *They are the brutal and violent world that you
> don't understand. They are unspeakable
> poverty, the temptation of a Companion to
> commit suicide last week, Olivier's mental*

142

*illness, Pierre's sickness. . . . I won't take
these things away from you.*

It would be so simple if you'd explain why these
things happen.

✝ *No. If you were able to understand all that,
you would be a little god. And I do not need
one.*

Then what do you need?

✝ *Your gift. Yesterday I told you that you have
enough light to rise above these thick layers.
In spite of these layers, and with them, give
me your love. Leap over them.*

After a few moments of silence:

Lord, it's a relationship you want, isn't it?

✝ *Yes.*

There's a certain weariness in this *yes.*

January 13

An image, a very strong image, of two points of light that intersect. One of the points, the strong one, is the Lord's; the weaker one is ours. When they intersect, sparks burst forth and then fall.

> ✝ *Do not worry about what may result from our encounter. The light and the sparks will come to rest in places that you would not imagine. Do not be concerned about it.*

January 14

From the very beginning of the Mass I hear:

> ✝ *My love, my love, my child.*

It's overwhelming.

> Give me some sign, any sign, that I'm not imagining these words. Please.

My neighbor reads the text of the day, from the Letter to the Hebrews: "Therefore, as the Holy Spirit says, 'Today, if you hear his voice, do not harden your hearts as in the rebellion.'"

January 16 and the days following

I sense that I have to put into practice and integrate all that the Lord has revealed to me, but still I can't restrain myself from telling him how much I miss him. He's not any less present just because I feel him less. No, not that. It's just that our encounters used to be so good and so powerful. He is here, and he is alive. I know that.

> As you wish, when you wish. But if you were to come and visit me as you did before, Lord, that would be wonderful.

Sometimes his only reply was:

> ✝ *I have already given you much.*

And:

> ✝ *I am here.*

The other evening, it was different. I was meditating on abandonment, on humility.

> ✝ *Enter the room with your head held high.*

What does that have to do with humility, Lord?

✛ *Enter my humility as you enter a room, with your shoulders squared and your head held high.*

I think I understand why Jesus tells me that. I refuse to believe (or perhaps I'm not able to believe; I don't know) that humility means bowing and scraping, or at least thinking you should.

We have to enter into your humility standing up.

✛ *Yes.*

I don't understand very well what he means by "the room," but he will explain that to me tomorrow.

Next day

Lord, are you going to explain it to me?

A few moments later I see a room filled with a thick haze or with cotton. It's all over the place.

✟ *Walk toward me; come closer.*

Are you at the other end of the room?

✟ *Not only there. I am also all this stuff that surrounds you. Bury yourself in it.*

What about humility?

✟ *That is what humility is, burying yourself in me.*

On several occasions in subsequent days it almost seemed to me that I was being enveloped in this thickness. Two serious problems were confided to me, both of them outside the Community. Once more I became faint in the face of human suffering and my inability to do anything about it. I literally buried myself in him as I went to sleep, entrusting to him two people who were all but lost. I felt myself physically enveloped.

Several days later

At Mass. I feel myself seized and, as it were, drawn by a point far, far inside me.

> ✝ *Bury yourself; bury yourself in me. Go all the way.*

February, March, April

The Lord is silent. Not absent, but silent.

I don't feel like an orphan, or like one abandoned, but like someone who's waiting.

One evening during a Eucharist in February, I told him that what we were doing in the Community was virtually meaningless.

His reply:

> ✝ *It is in this meaninglessness that you resemble me the most.*

If I had the time, I'd have to tell about all the little miracles we experience in the Community. But it takes time to do this, and when evening comes, I feel too drained to write.

We have just spent two weeks without Pierre, and everything went well. Of course, it was necessary to endure, to listen, to knock heads together sometimes, but I felt like I was being escorted and, in spite of the weight of these men, at peace.

December

The misery and distress of some people around me, rich or poor, affects me deeply. Some of them have inherited inhuman situations that they did nothing to deserve. They're so weighed down. It's so unjust. I tell him so.

> What a mess we're in, Jesus. We didn't ask for any of this, we don't deserve it. . . . It's because of sin, Lord, I know. Our sinful condition. But I didn't ask for anything; we didn't ask to be born. I don't feel any solidarity with Eve and her apple, none at all.

I'm filled with anger and revulsion, and with pain.

Jesus answers me calmly:

> ✝ *But I am in solidarity with you, with the others, completely. No matter what the situation, always. Do you understand?*

I was sure of it, Lord. You always turn everything around.

> ✝ *No, I do not turn things around; you do that.*

What do you mean?

✝ *You wanted to understand everything, to deal with it on an intellectual level. You talk to me about Eve. You would like to be the Alpha and the Omega. Once again, you would like to take the place of my Father.*

His reply immediately calms me down, but I'm not completely satisfied.

You always answer from the inside.

✝ *You will not get any other kind of answer. It is from the inside that I fashion my kingdom . . . and you certainly know from experience the marvelous things that can be accomplished even when you have to wallow in filth and mud.*

Yes, I know, I know. I have been living it for two years, but . . .

✝ *But do not be in such a hurry. One day in eternity you will know everything.*

I'm not in any hurry, not at all.

Letter of Paul to the Thessalonians: "Be joyful."

Here we are again, Lord. Joy, praise, no matter what the circumstances.

The priest expands on the theme, but I'm not at all in agreement.

What about the tears, what about the suffering that makes the sick cry out in pain? What about children in their hospital beds? What about your agonized cry from the cross, Jesus?

✝ *I have overcome death, all deaths.*

But you haven't wiped out suffering. The earth still echoes with the cries of those who suffer. I don't have to tell you. So what about this joy, Lord? What about this joy when Aunt Hélène weeps and is totally worn out after all those useless chemotherapy treatments? Absolutely not. What the priest is saying is full of lovely sentiment, but it's without flesh and blood; it lacks the real humanity that you yourself have given us. You know that, Lord, you know it better than I.

✝ *Nicole, it is not your joy we are talking about, but mine.*

Your joy is different?

✝ *Of course.*

What do you mean?

He shows me a piece of fruit.

Your joy, Lord?

✝ *It is the pit, the pit of the fruit. Do you understand?*

Yes. Your joy doesn't necessarily consist in smiles or happiness.

✝ *No, not necessarily. It is something else, something stronger and more solid. It is the certitude that comes from knowing that I am with you and in you. Do you understand?*

Yes. This joy doesn't sweep away obstacles.

✝ *No. It illuminates them from the inside.*

You always come back to the same point: your kingdom is on the inside.

✝ *Yes. Were you expecting me to say something else?*

What it comes down to, then, is that your kingdom is utterly "other," "different."

✝ *Yes.*

So don't be surprised if so few people follow you, Jesus.

✝ *I have never looked for the biggest number.*

December

Christmas is drawing near.

I can never get my Christmas shopping done early; I'm always in a panic as the day draws near. But it's a time when I feel like a child again and start singing for joy.

Jesus isn't absent, but I have the impression that he's letting me walk on my own two feet. It's as if he were watching over me from a distance, ready to run to my side if I call out. Distant, but not absent.

Christmas, Christmas. . . . With this childlike joy in my heart I feel forty years younger.

January 2

Mary's feast day.

Jesus tells me:

> ✝ *Be like her.*

You already told me that. You know that I'm trying.

> ✝ *Yes, I know.*

You want me to be ready to give myself, like her?

> ✝ *Yes. No looking back. Do not hold on to anything. Neither from the past, nor for the future.*

Could you tell me what you mean?

> ✝ *Do not try to figure things out; do not calculate. Go forward without trying to know what will happen tomorrow or at some future time. Mary did not say, "Yes, but." Get rid of the "but."*

It's difficult to give you the unconditional *yes* you want without understanding what is involved.

✛ *That is precisely the kind of* yes *I want from you.*

You know that's not easy, and besides, I'm afraid. When we follow you, Jesus, the way can become very difficult. I think about Mary and the sword that pierced her heart. When I think of her, I start crying, as you well know, and I begin to feel afraid.

✛ *Then you do not understand. Look at my cross. I have borne everything. Everything. And that makes it simple.*

Simple?

✛ *Yes. I have taken everything up on my cross. And so, if you are with me, nothing will happen to you.*

Nothing?

✛ *Nothing, provided you include me in everything you do. Provided you give me enough space so that I can be with you. There will be two of us, Nicole. So what can happen to you?*

January 3

Why are you so insistent, Lord. Why do you need this kind of yes?

✝ *So that I can make riches flow from your heart and your hands.*

Is that all! You surprise me, amaze me.

✝ *I will make you a queen. I promised you.*

Queen of your kingdom? Of the invisible kingdom?

✝ *Not only that.*

Yes, Lord. Do with me as you will.

January 5

Lulu and Chevalier show up at the Community. What a pitiful couple. They're filthy, and they stink. The two of them sleep in an old car. We get a heated trailer ready for them and some clean sheets, but on one condition: they have to take a shower.

Pierre looks at me.

> Okay. I'm going. Come on, Lulu, Chevalier.
> Let's get in the shower.

With Lulu and me it's the same old melodrama: insult upon insult. In order to calm her down, I suggest that she go and pick out her own dress and coat. On the way to the second-hand clothes store, I'm almost overcome by her smell. She never stops yelling at Jim and me as she picks out a dress, refusing a beautiful black coat that I had selected for her. "It's too dreary," she says. "I look better in green." So much for me!

It's a real circus—the three of us in that tiny shower stall! Chevalier is kind and gentle as he helps me with Lulu. He caresses her lovingly, and that both touches and comforts me. My heart is warmed, and things become easier.

Lulu, at last, is clean, calmed down, and finally happy with the change. While Chevalier finishes washing up, she cleans out the sink. She does a good job.

"This place isn't very clean!" she says.

My laughter is quickly tempered by the sight of a bottle of wine that seems to have appeared out of nowhere.

"Oh, Lulu!"

"A little bit never hurt nobody!"

We take away the bottles.

"Not even a little bit to go with the meal?" Chevalier complains.

"No."

The time has come to be firm.

The next morning, Chevalier was not in good shape. He and Lulu both had the DTs.

They didn't come back. They had chosen alcohol and couldn't do without it.

I'm disappointed, of course, but at the same time at peace. When I softly caressed Lulu's clean face, she broke out in sobs. Human misery had encountered tenderness and responded with tears.

"Oh, Lulu; you can cry, sweetie," says Chevalier. "I love you so much."

That was a piece of eternity for me. The absolutely clear certitude that Jesus loves us unconditionally, in spite of our depravity and our failures.

That evening in the chapel Jesus comes to me and says:

✢ *You see how easy and how simple it was.*

Pentecost

Jesus' silence weighs down on me. I've been spoiled. It's been several weeks now, even months. I try to accept this silence with docility, but it's difficult, and at each Eucharist I can't stop myself from telling him that I miss the sense of his presence.

> As you wish, when you wish, Jesus. But I'd really like to have you come back and speak to me as you did before.

I'm pestering him, I know, but I keep on.

Pentecost Sunday

Finally he answers me:

> ✝ *Nicole, I have not abandoned you.*

No, I know you haven't, but it was better before when we spoke to each other. I miss you, and I'm not going to pretend that it never happened.

> ✝ *But I am always here, close to you.*

Not like before.

> ✝ *No, but it has to be this way.*

Why?

> ✝ *I only withdrew from you a little to allow you to meditate.*

Meditate on what?

> ✝ *Your little notebook, my word. It is in the empty spaces, in silence, that you deepen a relationship. You already know that. That is how it is with Philippe.*

I'm so reassured I begin to cry.

Pentecost Monday

A Charismatic Congress at Le Bourget with 15,000 participants. I always feel somewhat lost in such a huge and animated crowd.

He returns.

> ✝ *Are you reassured now?*

Yes. I needed this.

> ✝ *I am not abandoning you. Make an empty space for my presence.*

A few moments later:

> Someday I'd like to go on stage and tell people about you. Is that all right with you?

> ✝ *Yes. There will be a time for that. But do not go too fast.*

July 2

We buried a Companion the day before yesterday. I can still see his smile when I went to visit him at the hospital; I can still feel his hand in mine when we prayed the Our Father and the Hail Mary. After hesitating for a few days I had asked him,

"Bertrand, would you like to pray?"

"Yes," he whispered.

He drank in each word of these two prayers and his eyes were amazingly clear. The cancer had spread throughout his body and the doctors wanted to try chemotherapy. The Lord took him.

"I want to return to the Companions," he said.

After talking it over with Pierre, we realized it wasn't possible.

"You will go home, to your own house, I promise you."

I wasn't lying when I said that, because we had often asked Jesus to take him home to his eternity.

That evening, in the Chapel of the Companions, one of the Companions and I pray before the Blessed Sacrament exposed. I relax in his presence and a feeling of calm gently overtakes me.

Your eternity, Jesus. What is your eternity?

✝ *Me.*

What do you mean?

✝ *Look at me.*

I do so, and at that moment the Host is a living man with wide-open arms who speaks to me. This isn't the result of my impressionability or my imagination. It cuts straight to the heart.

I see you, my Lord and my God. What love, dear Jesus.

At a time when I'm not at all expecting it, here he is, flooding me with his tenderness. I savor this moment because he's here, speaking to me. It's not that he returned, because he never left. But now he's here, speaking to me. I weep for joy.

Thank you, Lord. I needed this time so much.

✝ *I will never abandon you, I promise you. It has been rough and it will continue to be that way, but I have chosen you, little sister, little queen, my queen, the queen of my heart.*

I believe you. Yes, I believe you, and at this very moment I want to tell everyone about you at the top of my lungs.

✝ *There will be a time for that. Do not be impatient. I have already told you so.*

A few moments later:

Jesus, let's get back to what we were talking about. What about your eternity?

✝ *It is I, in this moment, but even greater and more all-encompassing. There is no break. Do you understand?*

Yes.

December

Philippe has to go to Lyons on business, and I'm going along for a couple days of rest. It's good to slow down and simply live. The return to Chartres is difficult. One of the volunteers who helped us considerably two years ago has turned out to be a big-time swindler. Suddenly the Companions and I are the talk of the town. We are front-page news in a local paper and become the focal point of a mess that attracts the scandalmongers. I can hardly believe the suspicions and questions that are directed at me, and I have to deal with people who are delighted to pick up the scent of a scandal in the making. An anonymous telephone call insinuating horrible things infuriates me. I'm physically beat and emotionally disgusted. It's not just the evil in itself that angers me; I am dumbfounded by the willingness of these poor souls to wallow in it, or to fabricate a rotten affair out of it.

Sunday evening, alone at home, my tears gush forth.

I entrust to Mary everything that I have discovered and have had to live through:

> Mary, this wickedness, these demons, take
> them all; bind them to the foot of the cross
> of your Son. Protect us, protect me, from their

attacks. Protect the Community, the little ones. Mary, Mary. I don't have any more strength. . . .

Calm returns.

December 12

✝ *I will make you a queen. I am making you a queen. My queen, do not be afraid of anything.*

Oh, Jesus, look at this mess—your humanity, our efforts. . . . I'm a pretty sorry queen.

✝ *Not at all. You are beautiful. You are a queen, my queen.*

What are you doing now? What do you want of me? Surely you can see what I'm going through?

✝ *I am building the pedestal together with you.*

The pedestal?

✝ *Yes, the pedestal for the queen, in order to lift you up a little bit, Nicole, and allow you to be seen.*

The pedestal? I don't understand.

✝ *You have overcome evil, Nicole. In order to overcome it, you had to meet it head-on. It is over. Like me, you have overcome it.*

Jesus.

It's a cry that comes from my whole being.

I don't resist. I know that I have overcome. I breathe deeply before resuming the dialogue.

> I believe you. It was quite a battle, but I know that I've won. It's enough to make me feel arrogant. Perhaps I'm being a little arrogant in telling you that I won.

> ✤ *No. As long as you fight together with me, as long as you leave me some room, you will not become arrogant.*

December 16

I talk to him once again about the queen, his "little queen."

✝ *I, too, give witness, Nicole.*

But you don't have to give witness. You have already given it, the witness only you could give.

✝ *I am alive. I give witness by making you a queen.*

The two of us give witness together, is that it?

✝ *Yes.*

And my witness?

✝ *Be at peace. Do not be afraid of anything. Show your joy.*

A little later:

✝ *I will take care of everything. Do not worry about it. I will see to everything.*

It's hard for me to believe you in the middle of this crazy mess.

✝ *I will do it.*

I believe you.

I have the impression that Jesus wants me to adhere to him totally, even though I may not know what he's going to do in this kingdom he's fashioning. Peace and trust are the part I have to play.

> May your will be done, Jesus. I'm in your hands.
> I'll try to be completely at peace. But you must
> know, Jesus, how these anonymous telephone
> calls upset me. So please give me a little time
> between calls to get myself together again.

> ✝ *I am your protector. They will not do anything
> to you. Be at peace.*

December

For several months now I have been noticing that it's easier for me to meet Jesus when I'm alone, whether at Mass or elsewhere. I've often wondered if this is simply because I'm too self-centered. I'd like to see myself a little more clearly. I'm alone in the car, driving to the Hermitage.

Jesus? Is it I who am too self-centered or might you perhaps be a little jealous?

✝ *Yes, I am a little jealous.*

Boom. My heart goes boom.

You? Jealous?

✝ *Yes. When we talk to each other, Nicole, it is important that you give yourself to me completely.*

You? Jealous?

It's still hard for me to accept these words.

✝ *Yes, yes. To give you more and to live in you more. Afterward you will only be richer because of this, richer for the others. Nicole, I really am a living person.*

End of December

These have been difficult and trying days. My soul feels fogged in and weighed down. I have the impression that someone is having a very difficult time. About all I can do is pray without really understanding what's going on.

January

✝ *Rejoice, Nicole. Rejoice.*

It's "Rejoice, Mary," not Nicole. I've misunder-stood, Jesus.

✝ *No. Rejoice, Nicole.*

A passing moment of uncertainty, but there is such a sense of peace in my heart that I know this isn't an invention of my imagination.

✝ *I will gladden your heart again, for my
   kingdom.*

I believe you, Lord.

Sunday

Isaiah 62:4: "You shall be called My Delight Is in Her, and your land Married."

These words go right to my heart, as if they were spoken to me. It's crazy.

> I already have a husband. You gave him to me, Jesus.

> ✝ *Yes.*

The Lord is in front of me, enfolding me.

> ✝ *I wed not only your being but your whole life, your family. It is even greater than that. The you I wed includes all the experiences I give you.*

The Gospel of the Wedding at Cana.

> ✝ *Do what she did.*

After thinking about this for a moment, I ask him:

> You want me to act as she did? Mary lives on two levels at the same time. There's the human predicament of running out of wine and the fact that you're divine. Mary knows that you can do

177

something about it. She doesn't know what, but she trusts that you will act.

✠ *Yes, Nicole.*

You want me to do what she did. I'm to live out whatever you give me to live out, without reserve, and I'm to trust you without knowing how you're going to respond when I call to you?

✠ *Yes.*

I meditate and pray a little.

Jesus, there's something that just doesn't seem right: it's too simple.

✠ *My love is simple. You make it all so complicated.*

But in a relationship, there's a give-and-take. What am I supposed to do? I can't just receive and let myself be led.

At that very moment the pastor speaks about the "feeble participation" that God asks of us when he works a miracle. He gives the example of the bread and the fish. They are so little, and the crowd is so huge.

I do want to participate, Lord. So what can I give? What do you want of me?

✠ *Your élan, Nicole. I have already told you that. The élan that leads you to go out to others, to me. The élan of your heart.*

That's not very hard. I'm happy to give it to you. What else?

✢ *Your trust. Like Mary, your trust. Your child-like trust that knows I am going to do something but is not concerned about the how.*

That will surely be more difficult at times, but I'll do my best. I promise you. We'll work together; you have my word.

✢ *I want them to see me, to know that I am alive.*

Several times during the Mass I'm shocked to hear:

✢ *My Father will come to visit you.*

To speak to me?

✢ *Yes.*

I tell Pierre about this because I'm so surprised by these words that I'm afraid of losing control.

"Write it down," Pierre tells me.

He doesn't seem to be at all surprised. We'll see.

January 30

Here I am, suddenly transported to another landscape. I leave home and the Companions, and now I am with eight rich and spoiled Americans on a two-week camel trip in the desert. Assekrem, Charles de Foucauld's sanctuary, is so beautiful it takes my breath away. I leave my little notebook with the brothers at Foucauld's hermitage. I feel both intimidated and stupid when I tell Father Georges what it's about. He doesn't seem in the least surprised. *Inch'Allah.*

Two days by car. I let myself be rocked and I dream. It hurts me to feel far away from Jesus. I put away my daydreaming and tell him so.

> ✝ *Leave your artificial paradise, your daydreaming.*

I do so and enter into the silence.

> I feel a great emptiness, Jesus. Not only the emptiness of the surroundings but a great emptiness between you and me.

> ✝ *Live in my presence.*

But the emptiness is empty, Jesus.

> ✝ *No.*

What do you mean, no?

✠ *This emptiness that you feel is not empty. It is the bond between my Father and his creation. Live in it with your prayers, like the brothers of the hermitage at Assekrem.*

Yes. Like them on their high plateau, between heaven and earth.

Explain this inhabited emptiness.

✝ *You are weaving along with my Father.*

Weaving what?

✝ *Why do you want to know?*

Why, in order to know.

✝ *Know what? What good will that do?*

February 1

Tell me about this weaving, Jesus.

✝ *It is prayer to my Father, toward my Father, with him.*

How is he different from you?

✝ *I am your companion. I go before you. I am in day-to-day life.*

And your Father?

✝ *Include the universe, the immensity of the world, in your prayer.*

Now, Jesus, I honestly don't think that is going to change anything, whether it's in Chile, in Russia, in Lebanon, or anywhere else. Just take a look at the chaos.

✝ *Let your prayer be completely disinterested.*

What do you mean?

✝ *Pray to enter into a relationship, without self-will. The same for the people I have given you. Do not pray to convert them or to reform them. Just pray for them.*

I understand.

✝ *Be like my Son.*

This time it's God who speaks. (I'm so frightened I hardly have the courage to write these words.)

Like your Son?

✝ *Think about the cross.*

Yes, you're right. He prayed for his persecutors.
He didn't pray that his persecutors stop doing
what they were doing. Yes, I understand.

And later:

How should I refer to you?

✝ *By my name.*

Well, then, God, I'm going to dare to ask you
this question. It may be stupid, but you initiated
this conversation. What's the use, or better, what
use is it for me to pray for a world and for situations that are completely beyond me? Here I am,
lost in your universe. My brothers are swallowed
up in your universe. It's crazy. And furthermore,
I don't see anything; I don't know anything.

✝ *Pray. First of all, you will enter into a relationship with me. That will provide you with a way
of entering into the vestibule of my eternity.*

I have time to meditate on this as we walk in the Teffedest,
but I'm still astounded. It's at once so immense and so
simple.

February 2

God, you gave us our intelligence so that we could understand. You're the one who wanted it that way. So then, you who are the Alpha and the Omega, you who have sent your Son to the world, take a look for yourself. The world is in trouble; it's a mess. Your Son died for us, but nothing under the sun has changed. What's the use? How do you expect people to believe in you? You know it's hard. We don't understand anything at all about your plan.

✝ *Understanding my plan is not the point. I am only asking you and all the others to contribute to it.*

So I have to put my intelligence on hold, on the back burner?

✝ *No. Just submit your intelligence to a plan that you do not understand because you will never be able to understand it completely.*

Partly, then?

✝ *Yes, but just a little bit.*

What do you want of us?

✝ *Contribute to my plan with what you have
and from where you stand. That is all.*

February 3

It's absurd. We really are nothing at all. I am nothing. A little grain of sand in this vast stretch of sand. Nothing. Minuscule. It's really quite ridiculous, isn't it?

✝ *Yes. You are this little nothing, this grain of sand.*

Nothing. It's hard for me to accept that.

✝ *In this nothing, there is everything. My All. There is me.*

February 4

How do we comprehend, how do we live and accept, being nothing at all?

✝ *With gentleness, patience, and modesty.*

What do you mean?

✝ *Like a work of art.*

What do you mean?

✝ *A work of art retains its secret, its mystery. Do the same for my universe, my plan. Treat it like a work of art. Accept that there is more to it than you can understand.*

February 5

A work of art. I don't like that. All these people, all these evils, all these distortions. How can you call it a work of art when there are so many disasters, such unhappiness, the death of innocent children? It's impossible.

✝ *My work of art is not finished. It is still going on.*

I think, of course, of Teilhard de Chardin.

✝ *Do what my Son did.*

What do you mean?

✝ *Live as he lived. He was just the son of a carpenter in a little village. Live as he lived where you are, and like him carry the world. Do not look for anything beyond being small, the mother of a family, the person who today is responsible for the Community.*

That's what you want of me?

✝ *That is what we want of you today.*

February 6

A work of art, with so much suffering?
Misfortune, the suicide of a child . . . so much
tragedy. I know, lots of books have been written,
so much has been said about suffering, but what
about the look of a person who is suffering?
God, you're all-knowing. Can you give me an
answer, a simple answer?

✝ *I share it.*

What do you mean?

✝ *I am in the suffering, in the look, in the agony.*

But, God, you need two to share. All those who
don't know you are unable to share and don't
know that you are sharing with them.

✝ *Nonetheless, I am there.*

But what good is that for them, since they aren't
aware of it? Since they can't feel anything, it's
no help to them.

✝ *What makes you so sure of that? Do not put
yourself in their place. Once and for all my
Son put himself in their place. He bore
everything.*

February 7

We have to put up with all this suffering.

✝ *No. What you have to do is direct it toward us
and do so with all your strength.*

February 9

I go to see the Little Sisters and listen to a talk on Charles de Foucauld.

Here I am all by myself, kneeling in the little chapel of the sisters. I have my feet in the sand, as I did in the desert. The presence of Jesus in the tabernacle makes me feel warm inside.

I think about Charles de Foucauld and his remarkable life.

> Did anything come of it? Do you want the same thing to happen to us, to me?
>
> ✝ *Carry the world.*
>
> But it's absurd. Why use me? What can I accomplish? What do you want me to do?
>
> ✝ *Nothing.*
>
> What do you mean?
>
> ✝ *Why do you always want to do something? Are you not already busy enough? Why do you want to do more?*
>
> Then what do you want of me?

✝ *Do not do anything. Let us do it.*

That's incomprehensible.

✝ *No, it is not.*

What should I do; or rather, since we're not talk-ing about doing, what should I be?

✝ *Carry us in yourself.*

That's all?

✝ *Yes. Like two treasures nestled down deep inside you. That is all.*

February 10

God, it's so simple. What you're saying is that
we complicate everything, even those who think
they're following you?

✠ *Yes. My Son and I are worn out by your use-*
  less efforts.

What do you mean?

✠ *You put so much effort into living your lives*
  and carrying out your projects that you leave
  no room for us.

The spirit of childhood, is that it? To trust completely and let oneself be led?

✠ *Yes.*

February 12

Along with the joy of knowing you, there is always the cross.

✝ *Yes.*

Joy and the cross, always?

✝ *Yes.*

I'm afraid of the cross.

✝ *Do not be afraid of it.*

How can one not be afraid, not fear it? It seems to me that you ask a lot of those you have chosen.

✝ *No.*

What do you mean?

✝ *The cross will not be heavy, because we will carry it along with you. We protect you. No one will be able to harm you. Believe it. Like a child, believe it.*

It's easier than I imagine?

✝ *It is even easier than the life you are now leading.*

Easier! . . . ?

✝ *Yes, because you really have no idea how*
much we surround you with our love.

Really chosen?

✝ *Yes.*

I'm reminded again, both in my head and in my heart, of
the spirit of childhood so dear to Georges Bernanos, the
poverty of Foucauld, the humility of Chardin, and of so
many others, both known and unknown.

February 13

Far from the silence and the beauty of the desert, I return once again to the intimacy of the family. I have the impression that passing from one planet to another has become less difficult. Probably it's because I'm letting go more than I did before.

February 15

Why do you insist so much that we not do anything?

✝ *When you become too active, you do not let our presence shine through.*

February 20

In his homily the pastor speaks insistently about two worlds: the present, ephemeral world and the true world that awaits us after our death.

> That's difficult for me to accept. I feel as if I'm being torn in two. I love this life here below, and I don't believe enough in the life that awaits me. The eternity that we will tumble into is hazy and vague. I'd like to believe more strongly, to be convinced in the depth of my being that joy awaits me. But you know how far I am from that.

> ✝ *Do not try to imagine it. You are unable to know it. Besides, you are mistaken.*

> . . . ?

> ✝ *There is no before and after. There is only the present—today, right now.*

> Eternity has already begun?

> ✝ *Yes, of course.*

A few moments later:

How do we live this eternity, this today? It's difficult, isn't it? When I'm making dinner, talking, reading a book—in short, when I'm doing the hundred and one things that make up this daily life, I can't be with you at the same time. Not all the time. It's impossible.

✝ *Simply leave the door of your heart open to our presence. Do what you are doing completely and well.*

And you?

✝ *Once in a while we will come and surprise you. We will meet up.*

February

A strong impression of the presence of Jesus. He even asks me:

✝ *How is it going, Nicole?*

Just as a friend would do. And then he continues:

✝ *Do not worry about anything. None of you need to worry about anything. Make your ways smooth.*

You mean to say that we should make the way smooth for you?

✝ *No. Simplify your lives. What I am sending you are just a few rough spots.*

February 26

I'd like to enter into your eternity serenely, just as I'm living now. That seems difficult.

✝ *No.*

What do you mean?

✝ *Turn the movement around. Do not start from what you do not know, from what you are unable to know. Do not start from what you imagine or fear after death. Start from what you see today.*

April 25

A telephone call this morning from someone who asks me to pray for her. She wants to remain anonymous. The simplicity and the tension in her voice affect me deeply. I promise that Pierre will offer Mass for her and that we will carry her in our hearts. The same day I receive a radiant letter from a friend of Uncle André who read my little notebook. She has cancer and is undergoing chemotherapy. She tells me how much the notebook is helping her. The letter is radiant because it reveals the nobility of a great soul, just like that of Thérèse. What a gift it is to be able to share on this level.

That evening at Mass I offer him these two souls and I feel profoundly heavy and sad. I confide their sufferings to him and I enter into a kind of somber universe: calm but somber.

It's difficult, Jesus, so difficult.

✝ *I know.*

I can physically sense that he knows. The words of the Gospel come to me. I mutter to myself:

It just doesn't work, Jesus. You know what we
need, you know better than anyone else, and yet

you want us to ask you for it. So we ask you and
at the same time we say, "Thy will be done."

I have the impression, ridiculous perhaps, that we are playing with loaded dice.

✝ *Pray, Nicole. Pray.*

To what purpose? You know that I can't do anything as well as you can. To what purpose?

✝ *Your prayer will make my collaboration
with these two souls even greater. Do you
understand?*

Do you mean that my prayer draws you closer?

✝ *Yes. Do you believe that?*

Yes. I believe you.

Summer

A family vacation with a friend. Everyone unwinds. Far out on an island without running water or electricity, we have the time to let the hours roll by. I was hoping that we would meet each other.

Aren't you going to come and see me anymore?

All I heard was:

✝ *Relax.*

And so I relaxed.

August

No encounters. I miss them. I tell them so.

> You come without warning, you go away with-
> out letting me know, and you leave me high and
> dry. It's difficult to accept this silence without
> any explanation. Moreover, as you well know, I
> feel like a post stuck in the middle of the road.
> I feel heavy and no longer experience the sweet
> delight of your presence. That's rather hard to
> accept.
>
> ✝ *Do not get upset. We are molding you. We*
>   *know better than you what you need. We are*
>   *not far away from you. You are our queen.*

So be it.

I accept their apparent absence.

On several occasions, as the Host is being elevated, I see
the face of Jesus. In the beginning it looked like the face on
the Holy Shroud, and I told myself it was an optical illu-
sion. But my overwhelming feeling of calm assures me that
it is not a mirage.

December

Is the little notebook starting up again? I don't know. I really am letting go. Jesus has not abandoned me, but it's more than two months now that I have been without these moments of eternity. What I feel so deeply is not his absence, but his distance. I accept it, but it's not easy. Since the initiative is his, there's really nothing I can do, but at Mass I often ask him to return.

> You've spoiled me a lot, I know. You asked me
> to put this little notebook into practice and to
> integrate it into my life. I'm trying. But, if it be
> your will, come and visit me. If it's not your
> will, I accept that.

He came back on Thursday. Of course I begged him to, but that's my way of holding on to the relationship.

Kneeling, he takes me in his arms and surrounds me with such love that I'm almost out of breath.

✢ *Now are you reassured?*

Yes. Can't you tell?

✢ *I am alive.*

I savor these moments, astounded and also profoundly happy. I believe that if the world came to an end at this moment I'd be happy about it. I feel permeated through and through by an inner peace.

> ✝ *This is what is waiting for you in my eternity.*
> *This is my eternity.*

I can honestly say that if that's what eternity is like, I'd be perfectly willing to die right now.

> ✝ *Do not be afraid. What I say to you, I say to*
> *all of you. Do not be afraid.*

And later:

> ✝ *I have chosen you. You are my queen.*

Yes, Jesus. You're starting all over again. It's too much, too beautiful for me. Set me down where I belong.

> ✝ *No. Nothing is too much for my kingdom. I*
> *have chosen you.*

Friday, the next day

✝ *Move easily, Nicole. Move easily.*

Move easily? What do you mean by that?

✝ *Move easily among the people that I give you,
among all the events I have put into your life.
Do not linger over them.*

Why? Tell me what you mean.

✝ *Move easily and you will become light,
peaceful, beautiful. Do not do anything. I will
act in your place. Let me act.*

You have chosen me to do nothing?

✝ *Yes.*

Then I'm of no use?

✝ *I will make use of you.*

Tell me what you mean, Jesus. Tell me what you
mean.

✝ *I love you.*

There I am, literally swallowed up in this love. It's almost
too much for me. I tell him so.

Let me tell you something, Jesus. I have missed you all this time, and now that you talk to me like this, I feel almost afraid of this immense love. It makes me feel faint, Jesus. It's crazy.

✝ *Yes, I know.*

You want me to let go.

✝ *Yes.*

I'm going to try. It's not all that difficult, and yet it baffles me.

February 7

All alone, I stop off in a little Romanesque chapel at La Grave in the southern Alps.

I speak to them.

> Your silence is a bit long and heavy. You don't speak to me anymore. I miss you.

Silence.

I insist. A reply:

> ✝ *We already told you. We know what is good for you. We are taking care of you in other ways.*

And it's true. I feel that help has never been lacking with the Companions. It's as if every time there was some need, they gave me the right person for the job.

> It's true. I know I've been spoiled, even though I didn't deserve it, but I still miss you. Why this silence?

> ✝ *In order to shape you. We are shaping you.*

What for?

✝ *So that you will resemble my Son.*

It's God who speaks, and this time I feel much less intimidated.

I'll never make it.

✝ *No, you will not. But we will.*

So what I have to do is let go, accepting even
this silence?

✝ *Yes.*

February 9

Still at La Grave. Philippe is skiing on slopes that are too difficult for me. I return to the chapel to see them, but this time it's locked, darn it. I sit down on one of the steps in front of the cemetery and gaze at the Meije Peak. The sun bathes the frosted cemetery, and I'm surrounded by the silence.

Thank you. This is beautiful.

And a little later:

How are you shaping me? And for what purpose?

✝ *Because you have to enter into the depths of silence.*

I'm a little afraid of silence. It's empty. It doesn't speak to me.

✝ *No. Our silence.*

What do you mean?

✝ *We are inside the silence. With you, inside the silence.*

But without speaking to me? Why?

✝ *Adoration, Nicole. This silence, our silence.*
We speak to you in a different way. Enter into
adoration.

What do you want me to do?

✝ *Nothing.*

But how am I to adore you?

✝ *By letting go. Do not do anything. We dwell in*
the silence, not you.

All I have to do is make room for you?

✝ *Yes.*

And it's true that they're there, both of them, and all I have
to do is close my eyes to enter into my soul. I go down into
it and they're there waiting for me, both of them.

I'm no longer afraid of God. It's terribly simple. The Father
and the Son and . . . me.

It's simple, very simple, too simple.

✝ *People make everything so complicated.*

Wait a minute. Experiencing your presence
right now is easy for me. What about the others,
those other men and women, some of them in
religious life, who struggle with doubt and
emptiness?

✝ *Once again you are complicating everything.*
At this moment we are not talking about the
others, but about you.

No, you're not going to put me off so easily. I have been blessed a thousand times over. You fell on my soul without warning and you made it your dwelling, while others who have given everything to you never find you.

✢ *We have already given you an answer.*

? ? ?

✢ *We have inscribed these people on your heart. We already told you that.*

What about Thérèse? All I have to do is keep her in my heart?

✢ *Yes. We will take care of her.*

Great.

February 17

For some time now the word *lamb* has been on my mind.

Lamb? What are you trying to tell me?

✝ *That is the way to meet us.*

What do you mean?

✝ *The man or woman who has been a lamb, an innocent one in life, is able to meet us.*

Is it necessary to have experienced this trial in order to know you?

✝ *Yes. You either have to have experienced it yourself or through others.*

That's the only way?

✝ *That is where we meet.*

How difficult it is. We have to be bruised to talk with you. It's crazy.

The beginning of March

I speak to them.

"Don't judge." That annoys me. How can we not judge? Like it or not, there is always light and shadow. To say "Everything is fine; everything is just perfect" isn't only false. An attitude like that can be dangerous or even idiotic.

✝ *Yes, you are right. Of course, it is necessary to judge deeds. But never imprison people in their deeds; never hold them there.*

What do you mean?

✝ *You are all in the process of becoming. Let us say you just noticed that someone has committed an offense. Fine. But look at the person and recognize that sometime in the future, sooner or later, that person will be able to choose the light.*

So I leave an opening. Is that what you mean?

✝ *No, you do more. You allow us to act with you, to look at these people with you, to understand them, to wait for them with you. Do you understand?*

Yes. What it comes down to is that I'm giving you a chance as well.

March 8

The Host is in our hands: fragile, vulnerable.

I say to them:

> You're so light and vulnerable in my hand. It's crazy.

I meditate a little on this piece of bread that is Jesus.

I hear:

> ✝ *Be light. I want you to be as light as I am right now.*

Since I'm not really sure that it's him speaking to me, I wait a little. There is peace. So it is him, not my wishing it or my imagination.

> Will you tell me what you mean? Maybe tomorrow?

> ✝ *Yes.*

March 9

I have some time for tidying up the house, and since I'm alone we speak to each other.

> Can you tell me what you mean by *light?* And by *vulnerable* too? That last word is a little scary.

> ✝ *Yes, light. As for vulnerable, do not be afraid. You know that we are protecting you.*

> Why light?

> ✝ *Do not carry what you do not have to carry. It is too heavy for you. You are not up to it.*

I don't agree and I tell them so:

> You created me, brought me into this world with my talents and flaws. To give an example, I was born with a certain degree of understanding and compassion. They were your gifts. And now I'm to put all this aside?

> ✝ *No. Do you think that we forgot about you the day after you were born? We were there at your side.*

> How does lightness fit in?

✝ *We are at your side. You feel, you see, you sympathize, but let us carry what is too heavy for you. Be light. We will do the carrying, and they will see us.*

They?

✝ *The people that we give you, that we lend you. The lighter you are, the more they will see us.*

March

I have the impression that you're trying to get me to live on two different planets. The first is that of the hidden kingdom: your presence, the little notebook, the little miracles that you let me experience. The second is that of the world: the thousand and one things that make up our daily life, the major and minor decisions (and there are plenty of them), and all that weighs down our human existence. I feel tossed from one to the other, and it doesn't feel very good. And why? Why the intimacy, the secrecy, of the kingdom?

✝ *So that you do not distort it.*

What do you mean? Why isn't this hidden kingdom revealed to everyone?

✝ *In order that the little may nourish the great. In order that the intimacy of the little notebook may nourish your life. You have to begin with us so that our kingdom may break forth.*

I understand. Yes, I think I understand.

The next day

You know everything about me. Everything, from all eternity. And yet you allow me to be free to choose to love or to not love. Even before I open my mouth, you know what I'm going to ask you. What a strange and yet provocative kind of liberty this is: determined and free at the same time!

✝ *Yes, we know everything, Nicole. But in a completely different way, not in your way. Neither your intelligence nor any human intelligence can know as we know. Our way of knowing is not the human way.*

What, then, is the link or the means by which we can catch a glimpse of you? There has to be one.

✝ *Trust.*

Nothing else?

✝ *No.*

. . .

To trust in you in the dark, without knowing.

✝ *Yes, but not in the dark.*

Why is that?

✝ *Because it is through trust that we enter into a relationship with you. It is the relationship that we desire.*

But what about all those who never experience this relationship? What about all the prayers that have gone unanswered?

✝ *Our answers are not your answers. You would like us to answer you in your way. At times our answers can be completely different.*

But then would we ever be able to understand them or even receive them?

✝ *Yes, but often it comes about gradually.*

I still have some questions to ask later. But first of all I have to assimilate what they're trying to get me to understand.

Very often I see a face coming into focus on the Host when it's elevated. Sometimes it looks like the face on the Holy Shroud, and at other times the face is inclined. The gaze directed toward me comes from far, far away, but it's still very close. I've already experienced something of this same feeling of sweetness when I've been embraced by the gaze of some people. That has happened rarely, very rarely, but the feeling is one of extreme sweetness.

I remain calm. I feel neither dizziness nor doubt, and when I don't see him on the Host, I'm not bothered by it because I know that he's there. It's all so simple and straightforward, but I'm still surprised by how calm I am. "Let go." Okay. I am letting go.

March 28

For a couple of days now I have wanted to ask which requests are good and which bad. "Ask and you shall receive." I feel like replying, "Not always!"

Several times I ask them:

> What are the good requests?

I know that they will answer me. I wait for the right moment.

After Communion, as I'm thanking them for the life they give me, the answer comes:

> ✝ *The good requests are those that come from your heart.*

And the bad?

> ✝ *Those that come from your plans.*

So what you want more than anything else is heart-to-heart?

> ✝ *Yes.*

April

Paris is a bit like Sodom and Gomorrah. Everything is possible; everything is permitted in the name of a pseudo-liberty and a so-called truth. I can't help feeling sick at heart. I don't want to take the Metro, so I walk for over an hour. That gives us time to talk. And, as is always the case when I'm feeling upset, the same thought comes to my mind:

> Look around you, Jesus. You came into our
> world. This is Holy Week, and you're about to
> go to your cross. You're going to take everything
> up into your cry of agony. But what a mess this
> is!

There it is. I'd like to be consoled by him who is still suffering. I insist:

> Don't tell me, Jesus, that this is just something
> between you and me. I see the others. I see how
> they're suffering. I hear them splashing around
> as they sink deeper and deeper. Look at them.
> Take a close look at them.

> ✝ *I know, Nicole. I know everything. But I did*
> *not come to be a reformer.*

What do you mean?

✝ *Be like me; do not try to reform them. You would not succeed anyway.*

Be like you? What do you mean?

✝ *Carry them in your heart. Place them deep in your heart, in the emptiness of your tears, and, like me, wait.*

Wait for what?

✝ *Their conversion.*

Once more, I don't have to do anything, just wait?

✝ *Yes.*

Will you wait with me?

✝ *Of course. Do not do anything. I will take care of it.*

December

Five free days. It's cold and snowy, but I'm with Philippe, the sun peeks out now and then, and there's a little church not too far away.

Finally I'm able to slow down, and since I'm often by myself, I go to see him each day in the church of Agentière. It's cold, and I don't especially care for the gold-encrusted baroque altar. You'd think you were in Austria. I'm taken aback, as I was in Patmos, by this "dripping" display of affluence. Jesus was born in a stable, after all.

For a long time now I have been wondering about sin and about myself. It seems to me that I have become reconciled with sin. I don't feel any guilt; at least I don't feel it anymore. Whenever I feel I have offended someone, I find a way to apologize as soon as possible. So where am I? Am I being proud, or is it just that I am lacking in my understanding of a basic Christian concept?

I talk to him best when I'm walking.

> This is day number two that I have come to see you, both of you, in your gilded church. Would you like to enlighten me?

Deep down I know that he will answer me, and at the same time, I know that he will answer me in his own good time.

I know that sin is serious, that sins are serious, and yet I don't feel in any way burdened with sin.

Am I being proud? Or am I totally mistaken?

The answer finally comes on the third day.

✝ *Sin is like prayer.*

I try to understand.

Tell me what you mean.

✝ *When you pray, you speak to me. You enter into a relationship with me. When you confess your sins, that, too, is a way of speaking to me.*

Jesus, for me sin is believing that we are God, that we are all-powerful. I don't think I do that. I'm pretty well aware of my limits, but I'm not very burdened by them. What good does it do to talk about them in confession, or even to mention them to you directly?

✝ *It is better when you say them.*

What's better?

✝ *Our relationship. The hidden kingdom.*

What do you mean?

✢ *When you tell me about your limits, you enter into a relationship with me and you hand those limits over to me. Do you understand?*

If I hand my limits over to you, if I tell you about them, then you will be able to do something with them?

✢ *Yes. You allow me to act, to extend you. You know what I am talking about; you have already experienced it: we are two. You do your human work and I extend it; I extend you.*

So it's not something negative.

✢ *No, not at all.*

My remark seems to make him smile.

February–March

It's neither absence nor silence. Nor is it the night. And yet . . . this friend that I was meeting so regularly has all of a sudden disappeared.

> We aren't in Lent any longer.

No answer.

> As you like, whenever you like, but it's so good when you come to speak to me.

No answer.

One day, in my exasperation, I say to him:

> Is it because I'm not humble enough that you don't come back anymore?

> ✝ *I did not come to visit you because of your humility.*

Bang! So much for me!

There are days when I say, "As you like, whenever you like," and actually mean it and feel at peace about it. And there are others when I'm really irritated.

> You're too much for me, Jesus. You come when
> I'm not expecting it. You make your dwelling in
> me when I haven't even invited you, and all of a
> sudden you're gone without giving any warning.
> It's a little too casual for my taste.

I have to enter into myself and be silent in order finally to
receive his reply.

✝ *I will show you other landscapes.*

Without you?

✝ *No, with me, but in a different way.*

And I know what he means: at the Community when Pierre
is gone and in my own home I sometimes marvel at the
way Jesus' kingdom is being fashioned. It's not very obvi-
ous, and yet it's very strong. For example, the tensions
among the members of the Community, which are suddenly resolved even though Pierre is not around. It's true
that when I'm all by myself with these men, I do let go
when I see that there is nothing more that I can do.

I'm often surprised to find myself saying, "You can take
care of this or that yourself." It's quick and off the cuff, but

it works. At any rate, I can't pick up an army cot and move into the Community!

It's true, I feel you at work all around me, even though I had nothing to do with it.

✝ *That is what I promised you.*

Are you really going to take me along with you?

✝ *Yes.*

March

I had the impression a couple of nights ago that the devil was prowling around me. I confess a certain reserve toward those who talk about devils. I'm sure they exist, but I think it's dangerous to see them everywhere. I believe it's better to live out fully the humanity that Jesus has molded for us and not worry about the world of angels and devils. Still, I have to recognize that I may be mistaken. Sometimes I can sense in certain souls a rigidity so strong it seems to be made of concrete. I'm almost ready to give a name to what's troubling them or causing their disequilibrium. I refrain from saying anything, of course, but at times I feel my heart begin to beat faster. It doesn't last long, but it comes on me suddenly and it's very strong, as if it were caused by something outside of me. When it happens, I immediately pray to Mary, and my heart stops pounding.

The other night, when I was home alone, I think I physically sensed the presence of the devil. After having spent an hour in prayer with Pierre and the Bon Secours sisters, I finally came home, happy to be able to sleep in peace in an empty house. I woke up in the middle of the night. Since I couldn't get back to sleep, I got up, walked around a bit, and then went back to bed. Suddenly I woke up with a start because I had just felt some kind of animal move over me, and I instinctively reached out to grab it. There was nothing there. It was a lot stronger than a dream, and I was revolted and terrified by some slimy thing that I had physically felt crawling over me. What most surprised me, however, was that in spite of my anxiety and the moment of terror I felt when I awoke, *I was not afraid.* In some way it didn't concern me directly.

Mary, protect me.

I went right back to sleep. I waited several days before telling Pierre about it. The memory is very vivid, but not at all terrifying.

April

"And the angel left her." I hear these words directed to me.

Is this the end of my little notebook, Lord?

✝ *I have already given you much.*

I have the impression that this is the end of the little notebook.

April

The silence weighs down on me. The felt presence of Jesus isn't there any longer. It's not the night, but nonetheless . . . Once more I implore him and I tell him this.

And then he comes and enfolds me:

> ✝ *I will not abandon you. I have given you the little notebook so that I myself might nourish you. Now you can continue by yourself.*

And you?

> ✝ *I will be with you, but in another way.*

I'd like you to be with me as I continue on.

> ✝ *You are strong enough now. But you already know that.*

Yes, it's true. Why are you letting me continue on all by myself?

> ✝ *Because those who notice this power are going to wonder where it comes from. The power that I am giving you is going to send them to me. Do you understand?*

Yes.

✝ *Then continue on by yourself.*

I'd need much more time to recount all the things and the encounters that come about partly, and sometimes largely, through my intermediaries. Without trying to program things or stand at anybody's elbow, the right people are there and what needs to be done is done. It all happens naturally. It seems to me that all I have to do is let the current of this little notebook flow out. It's natural and in a way so easy and simple.

I have a much easier time dealing with tensions. I'm more levelheaded and I clothe my sadness or my suffering with Jesus in a way that's almost physical. The difficulties of the moment aren't taken away, but deep down within me there's a center of peace. It's new and powerful.

May

✝ *We go from words to deeds. We promised you that.*